THE
MINISTRY
ANSWER BOOK
FOR PASTORS

THE
MINISTRY ANSWER BOOK

FOR PASTORS

ALMOST EVERYTHING YOU NEED TO KNOW TO LEAD A CHURCH

GARY L. MCINTOSH

BakerBooks
a division of Baker Publishing Group
Grand Rapids, Michigan

© 2025 by Gary L. McIntosh

Published by Baker Books
a division of Baker Publishing Group
Grand Rapids, Michigan
BakerBooks.com

Printed in the United States of America

All rights reserved. No part of this publication may be reproduced, stored in a retrieval system, or transmitted in any form or by any means—for example, electronic, photocopy, recording—without the prior written permission of the publisher. The only exception is brief quotations in printed reviews.

Library of Congress Cataloging-in-Publication Data
Names: McIntosh, Gary, 1947– author.
Title: The ministry answer book for pastors : almost everything you need to know to lead a church / Gary L. McIntosh.
Description: Grand Rapids, Michigan : Baker Books, a division of Baker Publishing Group, [2025] | Includes bibliographical references.
Identifiers: LCCN 2024043382 | ISBN 9780801094903 (paper) | ISBN 9781540904652 (casebound) | ISBN 9781493449026 (ebook)
Subjects: LCSH: Christian leadership. | Pastoral care.
Classification: LCC BV652.1 .M3933 2025 | DDC 253—dc23/eng/20250214
LC record available at https://lccn.loc.gov/2024043382

Unless otherwise indicated, Scripture quotations are from the Holy Bible, New International Version®, NIV®. Copyright © 1973, 1978, 1984, 2011 by Biblica, Inc.® Used by permission of Zondervan. All rights reserved worldwide. www.zondervan.com. The "NIV" and "New International Version" are trademarks registered in the United States Patent and Trademark Office by Biblica, Inc.®

Scripture quotations labeled ESV are from The Holy Bible, English Standard Version® (ESV®). Copyright © 2001 by Crossway, a publishing ministry of Good News Publishers. Used by permission. All rights reserved. ESV Text Edition: 2016

Scripture quotations labeled NASB are from the (NASB®) New American Standard Bible®. Copyright © 1960, 1971, 1977, 1995 by The Lockman Foundation. Used by permission. All rights reserved. www.lockman.org

Scripture quotations labeled NLT are from the *Holy Bible*, New Living Translation. Copyright © 1996, 2004, 2015 by Tyndale House Foundation. Used by permission of Tyndale House Publishers, Carol Stream, Illinois 60188. All rights reserved.

Portions of this book first appeared in *Growth Points*, a monthly leadership letter written and published by Gary L. McIntosh.

Baker Publishing Group publications use paper produced from sustainable forestry practices and postconsumer waste whenever possible.

25 26 27 28 29 30 31   7 6 5 4 3 2 1

CONTENTS

Introduction   7

1. Beginning Well   11
2. Finding a Ministry   23
3. Getting Started   33
4. Leading a Church   47
5. Pastoring a Church   67
6. Growing a Church   97
7. Administrating a Church   117
8. Leading a Board   123
9. Making Disciples   137
10. Designing Worship   151
11. Developing Staff   169
12. Finishing Well   183

Wrapping Up   201

INTRODUCTION

As one church leader quipped, "Pastoring ain't what it used to be." It sure isn't.

Years ago, pastors were expected to go to seminary, obtain the proper degree, and build a solid theological library (or at least have a good start on one). Today? Well, many pastors never go to seminary. Instead, they learn ministry in their local church. Likewise, an increasing number of pastors do not have a traditional seminary degree, preferring to rely on their personal ministry experience. And many younger pastors don't have much of a library . . . at least not on their office shelves. Increasingly, their libraries are found on their computers and tablets and phones!

All pastors, even those who follow the traditional route to ministry, face other changes in the way things are done. A constant flood of emails that need answering steals their time away from sermon preparation. An expanded list of expectations from congregants stretches their emotional ability to cope. Changing tastes in music and communication styles complicate ministry practices.

Introduction

Where do pastors go for help as they seek to do ministry in these changing times?

Where can a pastor go to find answers to basic but essential questions about ministry?

There are excellent books available on pastoral ministry, but most are too long and bulky for today's pastors to access. For example, the ministry reference works on my own bookshelves average just over four hundred pages each, and one of them is three volumes long!

Today's busy pastors and pastoral students are not accessing these wonderful volumes because the long articles gathered into longer chapters are more than their busy schedules allow. Few pastors have the time or desire to read through these books to find the help they need.

What *The Ministry Answer Book for Pastors* Is

Pastors today seldom read lengthy books about ministry or search through academic journals. Neither are they thumbing through Christian magazines (the few that still exist). Pastors now tend to read quick-reference materials such as blogs and short reference guides. And that's exactly what *The Ministry Answer Book for Pastors* is—an easy, quick, accessible primer for pastoral ministry. It provides short articles built on a question (Q) and answer (A) format about significant aspects of pastoral ministry. It is a reference guide that you can carry in your car, keep on your desk, or access on your electronic devices.

Do you need a quick sermon for a funeral? You'll find an outline in chapter 5. Are you looking for an outline of board responsibilities? You'll find a description in chapter 8. Do you seek insights on changing careers? You'll find ideas in chapter 12. *The Ministry Answer Book for Pastors* is a concise resource you'll use day in and day out. Its short Q&A articles provide an on-the-go guide for ministry.

What *The Ministry Answer Book for Pastors* Is Not

A reference guide like *The Ministry Answer Book for Pastors* can't answer every ministry question or delve deep into the theological, denominational, or theoretical aspects of ministry. Thus, *The Ministry Answer Book for Pastors* is not . . .

- a systematic theology, although some theology is, of course, included.
- a denominational handbook, although some information about denominations is found throughout.
- an excuse for a lack of personal research and study, although answers are based on solid study.
- a Bible reference tool, although some Bible references are included.

Keep *The Ministry Answer Book for Pastors* on your desk, nightstand, or anywhere you may need to access it during your busy ministry schedule. Scan through the short chapters and read the ones that catch your interest, or read one of the sixty sections each week over the coming year.

However you decide to use it, you'll find it a helpful resource for leading a church.

1

BEGINNING WELL

Role of a Pastor

The Bible uses three words to describe a pastor: *elder*, *bishop*, and *pastor*. Depending on one's church background, the role of a pastor is viewed in different ways, and one of these words is often emphasized above the others.

Elder: A translation of the Greek word *presbuterous*, from the root *presbus*, meaning "an old man; a person of age; dignity." The word as used in the New Testament appears to indicate the spiritual maturity of the person (1 Tim. 5:17; Titus 1:5).

Bishop: A translation of the Greek word *episkopos*, which contains the root word *skopos*, meaning "watcher, guardian, overseer." The word appears to indicate the person's leadership nature (1 Tim. 3:1–2; Titus 1:7).

Pastor: From the Greek word *poimain*, meaning "shepherd," and related to *poimaino*, "to feed or tend flocks." The word appears to indicate the caring nature of the person (John 21:16; 1 Pet. 5:2).

Q: What do these words imply about the essential roles of a pastor?

A: The three words represent the same person but different aspects of their role. Elder emphasizes wisdom, bishop emphasizes oversight, and pastor emphasizes care.

Q: What are the main responsibilities of a pastor?

A: To guard, lead, and feed the congregation (Acts 20:28).

Q: By what authority do pastors serve?

A: Jesus Christ is the Head (Eph. 1:22; Col. 1:18) and Chief Shepherd (i.e., pastor) of his church (1 Pet. 5:4). He has given (called, appointed) gifted pastor/teachers for each church who are to lead under his authority (Eph. 4:11–12; 1 Pet. 5:2–3).

Q: How many pastors should a church have?

A: Each church congregation is led by a plurality of pastors (Acts 14:23), but the Bible doesn't prescribe a particular number of pastors for a local church or how they are to function together. The Holy Spirit appears to leave room for churches and leaders to organize as best fits the culture in which the local church resides.

Qualifications of a Pastor

In any field, every position has a list of qualifications, and so does the role of pastor. Lists of these qualifications are found in 1 Timothy 3 and Titus 1.

Q: What are the primary qualifications for being a pastor?

A: There are fifteen primary qualifications for the role of pastor.

1. *Spiritual desire.* A person who has the internal desire or motivation to be a pastor (1 Tim. 3:1).
2. *Above reproach.* A person who is blameless (though not sinless)—that is, they are not open to attack from others since there are no grounds for any accusations (1 Tim. 3:2; Titus 1:6).
3. *Husband of one wife.* A person who is physically, emotionally, and mentally faithful to their spouse, if married (1 Tim. 3:2; Titus 1:6).
4. *Temperate.* A person who is seriously minded, with evidence of calmness in spirit and living a balanced life, as opposed to excesses of any kind (1 Tim. 3:2; Titus 1:8).
5. *Prudent.* A person who is self-controlled and demonstrates a wise and discerning attitude (1 Tim. 3:2).
6. *Respectable.* A person who is orderly, honest, and able to manage the affairs of life well (1 Tim. 3:2).
7. *Hospitable.* A person who has good relational skills so they are welcoming to all, especially to strangers (1 Tim. 3:2; Titus 1:8).
8. *Able to teach.* A person who can communicate God's truth accurately and clearly so people learn, respond, and act (1 Tim. 3:2).
9. *Not addicted to wine.* A person who has control over their appetites and is not fond of wine—that is, who is not a drunkard (1 Tim. 3:3; Titus 1:7).

10. *Gentle.* A person who does not insist on their own rights and is gracious and considerate (1 Tim. 3:3; Titus 1:7).

11. *Not pugnacious.* A person who is not stubborn, arrogant, or overbearing; rather, one who is fair-minded and willing to see a different point of view (1 Tim. 3:3; Titus 1:7).

12. *Free from the love of money.* A person who is not greedy or concerned for personal profit (1 Tim. 3:3; Titus 1:7).

13. *Manages their own household well.* A person who does not avoid responsibilities and relationships at home but lives out biblical priorities with love and wisdom (1 Tim. 3:4–5; Titus 1:6).

14. *Not a new convert.* A person who has been a believer long enough to have proven spiritual character (1 Tim. 3:6).

15. *Good reputation.* A person who is seen in a positive light by non-Christians and is known for being a person of truthfulness and integrity (1 Tim. 3:7; Titus 1:9).

The Call of a Pastor

Historically, a call to ministry was understood to be an immediate, specific, and often dynamic (crisis?) event that an individual remembered as the point in time when they were *called to ministry.* This view of the pastoral call has its roots in the Old Testament where God's servants (e.g., Abraham, Moses, Jonah) received dramatic calls to ministry. It's also illustrated in the Gospels and Acts with Jesus's calling of the twelve disciples and the apostle Paul.

The pastoral call is now seen as a gradual, growing conviction that God is directing a person to make their living from the gospel. This view has its roots in the New Testament Epistles and flows from the Holy Spirit's empowering of all believers with spiritual gifts. While all believers are called to a lifetime of serving God with their gifts, some people are called to serve God using their gifts vocationally as pastors (Eph. 4:11–12).

Q: What is a definition of call?

A: Erwin Lutzer defines God's call as "an inner conviction given by the Holy Spirit and confirmed by the Word of God and the Body of Christ."[1] This definition has three key elements. First, there is a growing desire in the mind and heart of a person who is motivated by the Holy Spirit. Second, there is confirmation by God's Word. Third, there is endorsement by others who have observed a person's ministry (see Acts 13:1–3 for an illustration of this).

Q: What are the principles of a pastoral call?

A: The following principles of pastoral call are understood as essential.

1. God's calling is unique to each individual.
2. God's calling requires some preconditions, such as the God-given ability to do the work, the God-given desire to do the work, and the God-given fit between the person and the work.

1. Erwin Lutzer, *Pastor to Pastor* (Kregel, 1998), 11.

3. God's calling includes two aspects:
- A *general call* to ministry—that is, a call to make one's living vocationally from the gospel.
- A *specific call* to a particular type of ministry and place of service, such as missionary, teacher, professor, or educator.[2]

The Ordination of a Pastor

Q: What does it mean to be ordained?

A: To ordain means to set apart, appoint, or commission. Ordination is the practice of a local church or a denomination to formally recognize persons who are called to the pastoral role.

Q: Who ordains pastors?

A: In churches that have a strong connectional structure with bishops and district superintendents, the denomination is responsible for ordaining a pastor. When a church is independent or part of an association of like-minded congregations, it is most often the local church that ordains. However, some denominations and church groups allow for either.

Q: What is the rationale for ordination?

A: Tradition is a strong factor for ordination, as it has an ancient precedent. Biblical evidence for ordination is sparse,

---

2. A study of 365 pastors reported that 66 percent thought their call to ministry was gradual, while 33 percent reported it was sudden and occurred at a time they could pinpoint precisely. See Alice R. Cullinan, *Sorting It Out: Discerning God's Call to Ministry* (Judson Press, 1999), 16. While this study is older, my surveys of master of divinity and doctor of ministry students in my classes at Talbot School of Theology continue to support these statistics.

but the public appointment of Joshua (Num. 27:15–23; Deut. 34:9) as well as the practice in the early church of the laying on of hands by the apostles (Acts 6:6; 13:1–3; 1 Tim. 4:14; 2 Tim. 1:6; Titus 1:5) offer some evidence of the practice.

Q: What are the benefits of ordination?

A: There are several benefits from ordination.

- Recognition of a certain level of education and qualification, often a master's degree.
- Recognition by peers from other churches—that is, other pastors know you've gone through a vetting process as they have.
- Recognition among a wider Christian community—that is, people know you've met established qualifications.
- Recognition of the secular community for service; for example, military chaplaincy normally requires a person be ordained by a recognized religious body.
- Recognition of the government to receive certain benefits such as a pastoral housing allowance.

Q: What is the difference between licensing and ordination?

A: There are several differences between licensing and ordination, although it varies according to the denomination or association of churches.

- Licensing is the act of a single congregation that gives a person authority to perform pastoral functions in the licensing congregation but not necessarily in other churches. In contrast, ordination is an act of a larger group of churches that allows ministry to all churches within a specific denomination or association.

- Licensing is viewed as an initial step toward ordination, while ordination is the final step.
- Licensing does not require an examination or a public service, while ordination does.
- Licensing is considered temporary; ordination is viewed as permanent.
- Licensing does allow one to take a pastoral housing allowance and to perform ministerial functions such as weddings.

Q: *What are some prerequisites for ordination?*

A: Three prerequisites are found in most church groups:

- The person seeking ordination has completed theological training appropriate to the ministry to which they are called. In some churches a theological degree such as a master of divinity or master of arts is expected. However, for some churches, simple evidence of a call by the Holy Spirit is acceptable.
- The person seeking ordination has one or two years of experience in some form of active ministry, which gives evidence of God's call to pastoral ministry.
- The person seeking ordination meets the biblical requirements specified in Paul's letters to Timothy and Titus.

Beginning Well

Q: What is the process for ordination?

A: While the process varies between church groups, it typically includes the following:

- Evidence of God's call or anointing for pastoral ministry.
- Education appropriate to pastoral ministry.
- The writing of a doctrinal statement of belief.
- An examination or interview with other pastors and denominational leaders.
- A public service of ordination, which includes the laying on of hands by other pastors.

Pastoral Ethics

Q: Are there expectations for how pastors are to live and work? Is there a standard of pastoral ethics that pastors must adhere to?

A: Yes, pastoral ethics are a compass guiding pastors through the complexities of ministry. From personal character to professional conduct, the call to reflect Christ's character is a sacred responsibility that impacts relationships, decisions, and a church's overall health. The following concepts are agreed on by most Christian leaders:

- *Pastoral ethics arise from the pastor's relationship with God. A pastor's ethical standards are a reflection of Christ's values—compassion, humility, and integrity—in their daily lives.* This foundation goes beyond rules, with actions grounded in the truth of Scripture rather than shifting cultural norms.

- *Pastoral ethics are strengthened as a pastor engages in spiritual practices such as prayer and studying God's Word.* These spiritual rhythms shape the pastor's personal character while they serve as a living example for their congregation.

- *Pastoral ethics are not just about right actions but participating in the life of the Triune God.* This unique approach transforms the pastor's heart, encouraging them to minister from a place of grace, truth, and relational depth with the Father, Son, and Holy Spirit.

Q: Are there general expectations or practices that pastors are required to follow?

A: Your denomination or church association may have specific ethical guidelines to which you must subscribe, but here are some general expectations:

- *Maintain integrity.* Pastors are the embodiment of the gospel they preach, making personal integrity nonnegotiable. Alignment between a pastor's belief and behavior builds credibility. Honest communication, keeping promises, and a number of other factors reinforce trust within the church and broader community.

- *Safeguard relationships.* At minimum, building trust requires confidentiality of conversations that are shared in private. Balance this expectation with responsibility to report issues like abuse or imminent harm to ensure safety without breaching trust.

- *Build boundaries.* Endeavor to treat all congregants with equal care, while keeping friendships within the church professional and avoiding actions that may blur relational lines. Treat all congregants impartially, showing Christlike love and respect. Boundaries prevent emotional entanglement, favoritism, and conflicts of interest.

- *Lead humbly.* Reflect Christ's model of servant leadership by empowering others and fostering collaboration within the church to honor the spiritual gifts, calling, and creativity of each member.
- *Preserve sexual purity.* Seek accountability through mentorship and peer relationships. Accountability partners and transparency are key safeguards that will help maintain purity and build trust.
- *Manage finances.* Demonstrate personal generosity and wise financial management as stewards of God's resources. Manage church finances with high integrity.
- *Avoid gossip.* Words hold immense power in ministry. Pastors are called to speak truth with love while avoiding divisive language.
- *Encourage congregational growth.* Guide the congregation toward spiritual and numerical growth by making disciples. Empower members to discover and use their God-given gifts to promote a thriving church body.
- *Balance friendship and leadership.* Healthy relationships within the church require balancing the pastoral role and personal connections. This balance ensures professional decorum without alienating congregants.

- *Rest and renew.* Embrace self-care and model sustainable rhythms of work and rest. Practice physical self-care through exercise and rest. A burned-out pastor is ill-equipped to lead others.
- *Prioritize family.* Give proper place to your family, making certain each member's needs are met. Make good use of time off and vacations to build a strong family.
- *Lifelong learning.* Continual growth in theology, ethics, and ministry skills sharpens discernment and moral clarity. Commit to lifelong learning, pursue professional development, and deepen spiritual growth.
- *Preach authentically.* Present God's Word truthfully, give credit for external materials, and avoid obsession with one topic. Honor the sacredness of the pulpit well.
- *Transition well.* When leaving a ministry, release former roles gracefully, respect successors, and refrain from undermining new leadership.
- *Foster unity.* Cooperate with community and church leaders to advance the larger kingdom of God. Strive to represent Christ well to the communities.

2

FINDING A MINISTRY

Prior to initiating contact with a church or making your interest in finding a church ministry widely known, it's wise to spend time preparing for the eventual process.

Decision-Making Grid

Q: How will I know if a church ministry is God's will for me and my family?

A: Before getting emotionally involved with a potential church, think about what God desires for you and your family. After prayer and discussion with your spouse (if married) and trusted advisers, develop a decision-making grid. Start by summarizing your . . .

- *Personal gifts and talents.* What are your strengths and weaknesses?
- *Personal experience.* What ministries have you done effectively?

- *Sense of call.* What position do you feel God is directing you to?
- *Personal needs and desires.* What do you feel God wants you to have in terms of such things as housing, schools, salary, and work for your spouse?

From your summarized list, determine four to six major criteria. What must be in place at all costs in your next ministry? These criteria become your decision-making grid. Trust God's leading as you develop your thoughts.

Introductory Materials

Q: *Are résumés, media, and websites necessary to find a ministry?*

A: Yes and no. Churches and pastors find each other through many avenues. However, most churches need to have some way of discovering information about your personal life, ministry experience, education, and a number of other items. Thus, it's wise to provide a résumé and other ways for potential churches to find out who you are, as well as your skills and abilities.

Q: *What should be included in a résumé?*

A: An attractive résumé should include the following information:

- Name, address, and phone number, making sure to include zip code and area code.
- Family information, including names of spouse and children, ages of children, and any information about your family you feel is important.

Finding a Ministry

- Job or ministry role preference and/or options.
- Education. Make sure to include all postsecondary education as well as seminars and workshops you've attended.
- Experience, including work history and/or ministry history.

Q: What other ways might churches find out about my availability?

A: Social media is a good way to introduce yourself to churches. Developing a personal website is also a good idea. As appropriate to the type of ministry you seek, a video of your preaching, teaching, or leading is profitable.

Initiate Contacts

Q: How do I get the word out that I'm seeking a church ministry?

A: Churches won't be able to consider you until they know you are seeking a position. Once you have developed your decision-making grid and introductory materials . . .

- Alert your network of pastors, friends, family, professors, and anyone else who may be able to help you connect with a church.
- In denominations with a strong connectional polity, networking with denominational executives and leaders is key.
- Sign up with online placement sites. They charge a small fee but expand the potential reach of your résumé.

- Practice patience and prayer. God works through the networks of relationships to get your name to the right people and churches, but in many cases it may take six months to a couple of years before you find the right church.

Screen Contacts

Q: When churches begin to contact me, how do I proceed?

A: Search committees will send basic information about their church, such as a general profile, bulletins, and newsletters. It's common for some churches to provide a booklet or online listing of detailed information, along with photos, diagrams, and statistics. You should look at the church's website, watch a worship service, and tour the ministry online. Then . . .

- *Compare the initial information with your decision-making grid.* If you have a match, proceed to next steps. If there is no match, write a letter or email declining at this time. If unsure, proceed to next steps. When there is a clear match, communicate your interest and desire to move forward in the process.
- *Request additional information as needed.* For example, budgets, annual reports, constitution and bylaws, and information about the community from the chamber of commerce.

Q: What happens when things get serious?

A: Churches compile a list of potential candidates and compare them to their own decision-making grid. After they

Finding a Ministry

narrow their list, if you are one of the few remaining candidates, they may request a personal interview online or in person. At this point, you should do your own due diligence to find out more about the church.

- Request the names and contact information of former pastors or people who were in the same position you are seeking.
- Contact these people and interview them. Most are happy to talk with you. Don't feel bad about doing this. Remember that the church is doing its own due diligence on you. They'll be interviewing those who know you and your ministry, and you should do the same on the church. Ask former pastors about their experience at the church. The way the church treated the last pastor is often the way they'll treat you. Ask a lot of questions and listen carefully, even to what isn't spoken.
- Call denominational executives to question them about the church under consideration. Leaders know their churches and will give you an honest perspective about the church and your potential fit.
- Contact pastors from other churches in the same town or region and interview them. Introduce yourself and let them know you're in conversation with a church in their community. Ask them what they know about the church in question. You'll be surprised about what they know and reveal to you.
- Be prepared for individuals (or a group of people) from the inquiring church to visit your place of ministry, perhaps unannounced. If you are one of the

final persons whom they're considering, it's standard procedure for them to come to meet you in person.

Candidate and Decide

Q: *A church has invited me to preach and interview in person. What is likely to happen and how will I decide if it's the church for me?*

A: Once a church has narrowed down its prospect list to a few people, they may ask the potential candidates to visit the church so they can meet in person and hear them preach. It's wise to ask if you're the only candidate or if others are being invited too. If you are the only one being invited, it's an official visit and a decision will be made by the church and you about becoming the next pastor. Before you accept the invitation, consider the following:

- *Be sure you want the position.* The church invests time, money, and energy to bring you there for a visit. If you know you won't accept the pastoral position even if they offer it to you, don't go. However, if you're unsure, feel free to accept, as it will help you decide.
- *Insist your spouse and children visit the church with you.* Having them along provides extra eyes and ears to make a good decision.
- *Arrange for as long of a visit (or multiple visits) as possible.* Any church or person can put on a good front or presentation once, but it's difficult to do so multiple times. The more visits, or the longer the visit, the more likely it is that you'll see the real church.
- *Expect that your visit will include . . .*

Finding a Ministry

- Preaching, if appropriate to the position.
- Dinner and visits in homes.
- Meetings with boards, committees, ministry teams, etc.
- Large group meetings with church people.
- Congregational question and answer time.
- Discussion of salary and benefits with appropriate leaders.

- *During the visit you should . . .*
  - Learn who the influential people are and spend time with them.
  - Listen well. Small comments reveal much about the church's needs and expectations.
  - Schedule time to rest. Candidating is a stressful time for you and your family. Take one day about halfway through the process to rest and reflect on what you've heard and learned thus far.
  - Schedule time to acquaint yourself with the community by visiting schools, malls, grocery stores, etc.
  - Schedule time to explore housing options. Ask a real estate representative to show you three to five homes in your price range.
  - Talk about issues you are passionate about.

Depending on the church's constitution, bylaws, and policies, the leaders or the entire congregation may vote the Sunday you are with them, or they may wait one or two weeks. Make sure you ask for an exact day and time when they will call you with the results of the vote. You don't want to be left waiting for them to contact you, as the stress is heavy.

If they formally offer you the position following the vote, here are some tips as you make a final decision:

- Find out the percentage of the vote—that is, what percentage of the people gave a positive vote. If you are told the vote was 100 percent, inquire if it was the first or second vote. You want to know the percentage of the first vote rather than a second or third vote. A 95 percent positive vote or more is a mandate to go unless you have some very serious reservations. An 85 to 95 percent vote is vague and it's your call. Less than 85 percent is most likely a no unless you have very genuine feelings otherwise. Remember, a vote of 85 percent or lower means 15 percent or more of the people don't want you to come. Having that many people against you from the beginning is a difficult challenge, so be sure of God's calling if you decide to accept.

- Ask for everything in writing. This is important, as you have made agreements on salary, vacation, sabbatical leave, study leave, and several other issues. Church boards and leaders come and go. The leaders who make the offer to you might not be in authority in two or three years' time. New leaders might not be aware of the promises made by the previous board. Having agreements in writing will help communication and avoid hard feelings later on.

- Respond within a reasonable amount of time. Once a church offers you a position, it's appropriate to ask for some time to talk to people in your life, spend time in prayer, and give additional thought to this important decision. But you can't wait too long to respond. One or two extra weeks is appropriate, but longer than that is inconsiderate.

Q: Should I tell my present team, leaders, or board members I'm interviewing for a new position? I think they're mature enough to walk with me in the process.

A: Be careful. Some people are mature enough to support you without any damage being done to your ministry, but others are not so mature. Letting others know you're thinking of leaving your position may cause them to pull back and question whether you're committed to them. In most cases it's unwise to let those around you know that you're considering a new position.

Q: What are some questions I should consider when making a decision?

A: The questionnaire "Finding God's Church for You!" is a helpful tool to use.

FINDING GOD'S CHURCH FOR YOU!

10 KEY QUESTIONS TO ASK YOURSELF DURING THE CANDIDATING PROCESS

1. Do I see myself staying at this church 5+ years? Yes No
2. Do I see potential for this church's ministry? Yes No
3. Do I sense that my spiritual gifts match the present needs of this church? Yes No
4. Is my philosophy of ministry compatible with that of this church so that we can work together? Yes No

5. Will I be able to adjust to this church's expectations, practices, and traditions? Yes No

6. Is the church facing opportunities for ministry that I am able to help it reach? Yes No

7. Does the church have a need for my ministry expertise? Yes No

8. Will I have enough credibility that the people will follow my leadership? Yes No

9. Am I willing to work hard at this ministry? Yes No

10. Does my basic leadership style fit the needs of this church? Yes No

---

Scoring: Count the number of yes responses. If your number is

9–10 Pack your bags. This is the church for you.

7–8 Strong possibility. Keep the door open.

5–6 Unclear. Ask more questions.

3–4 Unlikely. Consider closing the door.

1–2 A definite no. Send out more résumés.

3

GETTING STARTED

Leaving a Ministry

Q: Okay, I've made the decision to accept a new position. What is the best way to leave my current one?

A: Making a decision to move to a new role is only part of the process. It's also good to leave your current role well. In general, you should . . .

- Inform personal friends and key people in person and privately before any public announcement is made.
- Meet with the leadership board to make them aware of your decision, and determine the date and process for leaving your position.
- If you are a senior or lead pastor, draft a letter to the congregation explaining your resignation. If you're an associate or assistant pastor, prepare a letter to your team or major supporters.

- Make a public announcement noting the date of your final Sunday.
- Prepare your ministry team for your absence by planning the next several months with them.
- Be prepared for a farewell party. Accept all gifts and donations graciously.
- Create positive closure.
  - Focus on the positive. Don't use your resignation notice, final sermons, or other communication to express frustration, hurt, or anger. How you leave follows you for years to come, so leave graciously no matter how you've been treated by the church. Bless everyone. Speak well of the people and place you leave behind.
  - Communicate the difficulty of the decision. Share your heart with the congregation as you explain your decision. This is a good time to teach about hearing and responding to God's call.
  - Express appreciation for the time you've been with the church.
  - Offer hope for the future.
  - Share the exact date of the transition and the process. Point them to the right people (e.g., elders, deacons) for further information and questions.
  - Give permission for people to grieve. Don't try to fix everything.
  - Celebrate what God has done and what he's going to do in the future.

- Deal with feelings.
  - You and your family will struggle with emotions throughout the process. Give yourselves permission to grieve the loss of place, friends, and memories.
  - Some will see your leaving as a grand opportunity and rejoice with you. Others may see it as you abandoning them. Be gracious, truthful, and open.
  - Avoid clichés and glossing over tough issues from the past. You don't need to rehash old wounds, just admit there were some tough challenges in the past.
  - Allow for different emotions to surface openly. Listen to the words and emotions of others while also giving yourself freedom to share your own feelings.
  - Calibrate appropriate responses. Here are a few things you might say to others: "I'm looking forward to new challenges, but it doesn't make it any easier leaving you." "Leaving you is sad for me and my family too." "We all move on sometime, but it's not easy."
  - Meet with groups of people or individuals who ministered to you over the years. Express your appreciation and share how they've impacted your life.
  - Give permission for others to help and talk with you about your move. Allow people to provide things like meals and childcare while you pack or to assist you in other ways.

- Attempt to mend broken relationships. It's easy to walk away from broken relationships when moving to a new ministry, but it might be wise to meet one last time in an attempt to gain healing. If the relationship is mended, you'll go on to the next ministry with relief. And if it isn't healed, at least you'll know you tried your best.
- Keep your children high on your priority list. Consider how they are feeling and handling the transition too. Help them say goodbye to their friends, neighbors, and family.
- Don't stay long. Four to six weeks after you announce your official resignation is about the limit, although some stay longer. Lingering as a lame duck hinders the church from moving forward and makes it difficult for you and your family to have a healthy transition.
- Put a lid on your delight. Your new position may come with a fresh challenge, more money, and freedom to innovate, but don't make the church you're leaving feel inferior.
- Finish what's doable, delegate what you can, and let go of the rest. Try not to take on new work while you're in the process of leaving.
- Relax and remind yourself of all the reasons you felt God was calling you to make a change. Premove jitters are natural.
- It's normal to drag through the weeks before you leave. After accepting a new call or appointment, your mind will drift ahead to the new opportunity instead of what you are leaving behind.

The First Year

Q: When a new president is elected, there's a lot of talk about their first hundred days in office because it sets the tone for their administration. Is that true for pastors too?

A: Yes, it is. But for pastors it's the first year rather than just the first three months. The first year is often called the "honeymoon" and, like in a marriage, is crucial for determining future vitality. The roots of future success and failure are found in the first year of a pastorate. Handle the entry into a new church well and it will go far in helping you succeed for years to come. Do it wrong and you may not last more than a year or two.

Q: An older pastor whom I respect told me it's best not to change anything during the first year at a church. Do you agree with that advice?

A: No, I don't. In the first year of ministry you establish a modus operandi (method of operation) that creates a tone for the remainder of your service in that church. If you don't change anything, it'll create an expectation you'll be a passive leader. That's not good. People know that a new pastor brings new ways of doing ministry, so take action and change some practices, approaches, or processes. But be careful not to get yourself fired by changing too many things all at once or making many major changes right away. Keep the long view in view.

Q: So, if I take some action, what should I do the first year? How should I begin?

A: Each church is different, but a practical approach is to develop a plan. Here are some ideas to get started.

- *Focus on doing your job well.* If you're the preaching pastor, do the best you're capable of doing. If you're an associate or assistant pastor, complete your work with excellence.
- *Focus on relationships.* Connect with your team of leaders. Spend special time with staff, members of the board, and ministry leaders. As you identify informal leaders, make space for them too. Try to understand the passions, personality, gifts, and style of each person you encounter. As time allows, spend it with people in general.
- *Be there for major life events* such as funerals and weddings. Serving people well during major life events does wonders to build your credibility.
- *Walk slowly through the lobby.* Meet and greet people and listen to their words and hearts.
- *Make some reasonable changes.* Set your own office hours, organize a planning meeting for the first year, and insert some of your ideas into the calendar. Adjust the worship service order somewhat to fit your approach and style. Do enough that people see you're an active leader rather than passive.

Q: The previous pastor of my church retired but still attends on Sundays. I've heard horror stories about former pastors undermining the ministry of a new pastor. How should I handle this situation?

A: You're right, there are lots of stories about former pastors being the proverbial burr under the saddle of a new pastor. But there are also many good stories of former pastors supporting the new pastor. My recommendation is to invite them onto your team. I'm not saying they need to be part of your board meetings, but it would be appropriate if you could meet with them about once a month for a meal. Welcome them as a friend, share your hopes and dreams for ministry in the church, and ask for their advice, insights, and input. Retired pastors desire to be respected and useful. By bringing them onto your informal team of advisers, you'll earn their trust and find them to be a valuable resource.

Philosophy of Ministry

Q: I'm confused. What is a philosophy of ministry?

A: Whether they know it or not, every pastor has a philosophy of ministry, which is simply a picture of what you want to *be* and how you want to *do* ministry.

If you haven't already developed a philosophy of ministry, use the first year to think through two questions: (1) How do I perceive myself in ministry (or what do I want to be)? For example, you might see yourself as a pastor or evangelist or youth pastor or discipler or some other role. (2) How do I see that role functioning? For instance, you might desire to be a pastor, but there are many ways for the role of pastor to function.

Once you determine what you want to be (this is the easy part), write a statement of how you see this playing out in real time (this is more difficult). For example, if you see yourself as a pastor, within that role you might see yourself functioning as a preacher, counselor, caregiver, or visionary leader. The more you can express how you see yourself functioning in your given role, the closer you'll be to finding your philosophy of ministry.

Q: I'm a young pastor and not quite sure how I want my ministry and church to function. There are so many models and options today, how do I figure out what my philosophy is?

A: There are numerous models for pastoral ministry today. As you begin your ministry, realize that whatever philosophy of ministry you have now is likely to change. Most pastors start out imitating some respected pastor. You may borrow that person's philosophy of ministry for a time, but your views will change over time.

- *A philosophy of ministry is discovered over time.* The more experience you have, the more clarity you'll have about how to do ministry and how ministry is accomplished with your individual gifts.

- *A philosophy of ministry is discovered through trial and error, especially crisis events.* You might begin ministry with a particular idea for how to handle conflict, but after you've worked through several conflict situations in a local church, your perspective will change and you'll modify your philosophy of ministry accordingly.

- *A philosophy of ministry is discovered through ministry ups and downs, successes and failures.* A good friend of mine used to say, "You get wisdom in one of two ways: You learn from others' mistakes or you learn from your own mistakes." He's right. Young pastors start out with an untested philosophy about how to practice church ministry. In time, their philosophical approach is tested in the real world of church ministry. Mistakes are made, failures are experienced, and wisdom is gained. It's a natural process toward a learned philosophy of ministry.

- *A philosophy of ministry becomes clear in retro-spect.* The longer you are in pastoral ministry, the more you are able to look back to see where God has blessed your life and ministry. You can observe where you used your gifts well and where you weren't as successful. With time you learn your strengths, your gifts, and what you are good at. Some ministry approaches work for you and others don't. Give yourself a measure of grace as you seek out the best philosophy of ministry that fits you. It will become clear in time.

Q: Isn't there just one philosophy of ministry—that is, a biblical philosophy? The Bible gives us instructions about ministry, so how is it possible to have different philosophies of ministry?

A: What you say is true in part. The Bible does give us instructions on doing church ministry. Yet, the Bible tells us *what* to do more than *how* to do it. For example, we're instructed to worship in spirit and truth (John 4:24), but the Bible doesn't tell us what style of music to use. We're told to do things "decently and in order" (1 Cor. 14:40 ESV), but the Bible doesn't give us a precise order of service. The same is true for almost everything about the local church. We're told to pray, preach, teach, gather, and so much more, but often the way we do these things is left up to us. The *how* is where differences arise regarding philosophy of ministry.

Q: What are some of the major contributing factors to an emerging philosophy?

A: There are untold factors that go into the development of a philosophy of ministry, but here are some major ones:

- Sense of call
- Church background
- Role models
- Education
- Gift mix
- Personality
- Experience
- Biblical understanding of the church

Building Trust

Q: I've read that trust between the pastor and people in the congregation is crucial to future success. What do you think?

A: Loving relationships are foundational to focused, faithful, and fruitful ministry. Paul points out the crucial nature of relationships by calling attention to the reality that people follow leaders as they follow Christ. He commands, "Be imitators of me, just as I also am of Christ" (1 Cor. 11:1; see also 1 Cor. 4:16; Phil. 3:17).

Regrettably, some pastors struggle to create meaningful relationships with people, and consequently trust is undermined. Remember, with every action you are doing one of two things: establishing trust or creating mistrust. Here are some insights and tips that you may find useful as you seek to build trust with your people.

- *Initiate good conversations.* One of the main ways to build trust is through good conversations. You may find it helpful to actually track the relational encounters you have with people in your church. How many lunches do you have each week? What do you talk about? What do you learn about the people? As you initiate good conversations, you'll build a certain level of energy to enable trust to develop.
- *Follow the social mores.* It's essential to follow the basic manners and customs of a church to establish, build, and maintain credibility. Social mores are the customary or acceptable ways to behave in a community. While you may think some of the customs in your church are silly, it's best to follow them until you gain enough trust to challenge them.
- *Keep your promises.* We've all experienced a time when someone made a promise and then failed to follow through. Failing to return phone calls or answer emails is a regular occurrence but a bad communication skill. If you habitually stall on replying to others, it undermines trust in your leadership.
- *Take your time.* Time and taking time are essential for connection and relationship building. In the first few years of church ministry, people are checking you out to see if you're trustworthy. They need to know from experience that they can trust you with their hearts—their deep feelings, hurts, and pains. This only comes after they've seen you up close and personal in real ministry situations, so give it time.
- *Don't overschedule.* As you build relationships, gauge your time wisely and don't overschedule. Make

room for interruptions. Remember, these are not interruptions but God-ordained time for building relationships.

- *Ask others for advice.* If you go about the work of pastoring as though you don't need others, it indicates you don't value others in the work. Asking for advice shows that you respect others' gifts, knowledge, feelings, and experience.
- *Connect on an emotional level.* This involves asking a lot of questions and listening to what people say. Use words and phrases like "Why?," "I think there's a story behind that," and "Tell me more." This shows that you care for others and are willing to listen to what they think before recommending changes. Be sure to take notes as you listen, for it conveys your care.

Develop Credibility

Q: Leadership is based on trust between a leader and his or her followers. It is a truism that few will follow a person they do not trust. So, how does a leader build credibility?

A: Credibility is built on the foundation of integrity. Followers must have confidence in the person who leads them, and confidence is established when a leader has integrity. What, then, is integrity?

The Bible uses several different words for integrity, including blameless, perfect, complete, finished, pure in heart, sincere, and truthful. In most occurrences integrity carries the meaning of being genuine, honest, and upright. Thus, a person of integrity is one who is honest, truthful, and sincere.

A leader of integrity is above suspicion and does his or her best to accomplish what God requires with simple sincerity from a pure heart. Credibility is based on . . .

- *Individual accomplishments.* A leader gains credibility by contributing results that are valued by people in the church. What is honestly valued depends on the organizational culture. For example, a pastor might be appointed to a church with a mandate to increase the evangelistic outreach. While this is an important aspect of a healthy church, it may not be what the people really value. If the church culture values care of members over evangelism of outsiders, successfully developing an outreach program may not increase the pastor's credibility. Credibility is only increased when results match the church's real values.
- *Individual situation.* Unfortunately, a pastor's credibility is not based solely on actual accomplishments but on others' perceptions. Each pastor carries a reputation that is based partially on past results as well as on their current actions within a church. People in a church, however, rely on their own understanding and perceptions as they assign credibility to leaders. In the extreme, people may give credit or blame to a pastor based on how they perceive each success or failure. Their perceptions are often determined by the leader's relationship with them.
- *Individual relationships.* The quality of relationships a pastor has with individuals in the church is a major determiner of how much credibility he has. With better relationships, a pastor's reputation and current

actions are likely to be viewed more favorably. With better relationships, a pastor is also more likely to get things done. Thus, developing good relationships with others in the church is a key aspect of building credibility.

4

LEADING A CHURCH

Lead Yourself

Q: What is the major challenge of leadership?

A: The major challenge of every leader is leading themselves! Pastors can't lead until they've led themselves. What got them to where they are today will not get them to where they want to be tomorrow. This means the truly faithful pastor never graduates but is a perpetual student. They know they must continually upgrade their knowledge, skills, and abilities on a regular basis. It's true! Growing churches are led by growing pastors.

Q: Why should I lead myself?

A: Here are five reasons you should lead yourself.

1. People holding the position of pastor in today's or tomorrow's churches need to upgrade their

knowledge and skills on a regular and continuing basis. Once upon a time (like many mythological stories begin), a three- or four-year seminary or Bible college education prepared a pastor for a forty-year ministry career. The word seminary is from the Latin *seminarium*, meaning "seed bed." The idea is that a seminary education provides the seeds that will grow into a lifelong ministry. This was true for many years when life changed at a slower pace. In the rapid-paced world pastors function in today, however, it's not possible. Changes take place at breakneck speed. Each week, innovative technology emerges to challenge the way we relate, communicate, organize, and plan. The passive learner quickly falls behind. At best, today's seminary or Bible school education prepares pastors for ten years of ministry. Remember, you must reeducate yourself every decade to stay current with life and ministry.

2. You must take responsibility for your own growth and development. It would be helpful if your church took responsibility to help you learn and grow. Regrettably, this rarely happens. While businesses spend billions of dollars a year to train and retrain their people, only the best of the best churches invest any money in the training of their pastors. If you don't take responsibility for your own growth and development, likely no one will. Thus, ask yourself questions: Do I know what I'm doing? Do I have a sense of where I'm going? Do I feel out of touch with ministry today? Stop being passive about your own

Leading a Church

personal growth. Remember, you can't shrink your way to leadership.

3. The broader the range of your responsibilities, the more significant your continued training becomes. While it's critical that continuing education be encouraged for children's pastors and youth pastors, it's doubly important that senior pastoral leaders keep learning too. Lead pastors (senior or solo) regularly are bogged down wearing so many hats that they neglect their own development. Progress begins when you take time to invest in yourself.

4. You must have a deliberate self-improvement plan. Such a plan must include getting away from your church and ministry—the daily, weekly, and monthly routine—so you can stand back and view it from a wider and deeper perspective. Plan and calendar your personal growth as you do your normal work schedule. Such a plan isn't easy and it takes self-discipline. Open your calendar right now. Are there scheduled appointments for your personal development? Do you see any scheduled interviews? Remember, you won't improve until you have a personal improvement plan.

5. You can't manufacture the desire to learn. The motivation for continual self-improvement must originate from inside yourself. No hodgepodge of learning techniques, books, blogs, or classes will take the place of your personal desire to learn, grow, and advance in your field of ministry. Pastors who can't motivate themselves can't be motivated by any outside forces.

Q: What are the best practices to lead yourself?

A: Pastors lead themselves well by employing some of the following best practices.

- *Determine your life purpose.* Close your eyes and imagine you're at your funeral. Now, this is not a morbid exercise—just allow yourself to think about what you hope people will say about you at your funeral. Then, in twenty-five words or less, summarize what you hope you'd hear into an overall life purpose or mission statement. Now, write down your life purpose in a notebook or on your computer. Read it out loud. It sounds like growth, right? Where do you need to grow? In what ways do you need to develop? How must you improve in your skills and relationships to fulfill your life purpose?

- *List your ten most important things.* Make a list of the ten things in life that are most important to you right now. It may help to divide up the important things into categories like spiritual/devotional, spouse/family, health/exercise, wealth/retirement, career/ministry, plus a miscellaneous one. For each item, write down two or three ways that you can advance or enhance it. These become self-improvement goals. As you work on them, you are leading yourself.

- *Get to know yourself.* What are your unique strengths? Your unique weaknesses? What makes you angry, sad, or worried? How do you define success? Once you've determined the answers to these questions, you'll be tempted to work on improving your weaknesses. While that is not a bad decision, it's not the wisest one. You're unlikely to make your weaknesses a strength. Wisdom from successful leaders points out it's best to work on growing your strengths while staffing people around you to care for your weaknesses. What are your top two or three strengths? How can you begin to design a growth program to enhance those strengths?

- *Build yourself broadly.* Fruitful pastors of the future must be well-rounded people. You might put it this way: Knowledge enriches knowledge, and the more the variety, the greater the enrichment. A lead pastor must be a specialist plus—that is, he must be a specialist with a wider body of knowledge. Ask yourself, Do I have time for random soul searching? Do I have time for self-renewal not directly related to my ministry? Do I have time for outside activities (e.g., art, sports, reading, music) that will enlarge my personhood? In the end, do you have a plan to strengthen your cultural enrichment and renewal that broadens your entire personhood as well as your skills?
- *Manage your time and energy.* How well do you manage your use of time? How well do you manage your energy (health, fitness, rest)? How well do you manage your relational time (family, friends, vacations, days off)? Here's the truth: Time management is just self-management. No one can honestly manage time. Everyone has the same amount—168 hours a week! Here's a tip: Make space on your calendar for personal development.

Lead the Church

Q: *We're holding our own in today's changing environment. Everything* seems *to be moving along well, but is it?*

A: Today, pastors and other church leaders get surprised by challenges that threaten their success or even their continuation of ministry. Danger signals go unnoticed or ignored because they appear in subtle ways rather than in drastic forms that garner attention. What are some of these common leadership pitfalls? Research has found several common obstacles. Let's call them "Leadership's Seven Deadly Sins."

- *A Lack of Direction.* Where is your church heading? Is there a clear understanding of your mission and how to get there? When you and other church leaders take a hard look at your basic model of ministry, ask yourself how long it has been since your systems and procedures were reviewed to see if they mesh with the overall mission.
- *A Lack of Follow-Through.* If your church has a solid mission and direction, great! Now, how well are you following through on implementing it? It takes more than a nice sounding mission statement to see growth in a church; it takes application—action.
- *A Lack of Assimilation.* Church leaders rejoice in the large number of guests who attend worship services. Guests are good, of course. But are they returning? Are they staying? Are they getting connected? Is your welcome system working?
- *A Lack of Communication.* All too often, church leaders assume that everyone else in the church

operates from the same level of dedication, commitment, and knowledge. They are shocked to discover that assumption isn't correct. Communication of the church's mission, overall direction, and goals is a never-ending job. They must be declared weekly before all people in the congregation begin to understand, believe, and embrace them.

- *A Lack of Delegation.* Teaching on spiritual gifts as well as the believer's duty to minister is common in most churches. What, though, is the reality? Is the work of ministry being shared with others? Are you doing things that others could do better? Are new leaders allowed to emerge?

- *A Lack of Smart Work.* It's not about working harder. Pastors, on average, work over sixty hours a week. The issue is learning to work smarter. Where do you put your time? Is it productive? Are you working from your strengths or out of your weaknesses?

- *A Lack of Dissatisfaction.* It's important to always have some dissatisfaction. Complacency is the biggest danger in a church that appears to be doing well. Once all the major challenges and goals are addressed, people tend to sit back and rest. This leads to rearranging tasks and priorities to just get by. Opportunities for new growth and outreach are ignored. Fresh challenges are neglected. Here are some signs of the sin of complacency:

  - Leaders feel comfortable and demonstrate less willingness to take appropriate risks.

  - A lack of interest in what's really happening in the various fields of church ministry.

- A feeling that "We tried that before and it didn't work, so it won't work now either."
- A realization that everyone is thinking alike or, even worse, that no one is thinking at all.
- An inward focus that neglects evangelism and outreach into the community.

Which of these deadly sins do you see in your church? Pick one and work on it this year.

Develop Vision

Q: *I hear a lot of talk about vision but am not sure what it is. Can you explain vision in a simple way so I can understand it?*

A: Vision is an ability to foresee or perceive something that is not visible. It is bringing to mind a mental picture of a preferable future. Vision is a picture of what God wants to do in and through us in our place of ministry. Vision is a prompting to do what God wants and is characterized by the following actions:

- *Inspires*. It transcends the day-to-day work of just doing a job to creating a place of impact and change.
- *Challenges*. Think of Dr. Martin Luther King Jr. saying "I have a dream." A simple dream of Black and white Americans living together in harmony. Simple, clear, and powerful!
- *Sustains*. It makes sense to the people. Vision is evaluated, critiqued, and fine-tuned until it motivates the followers.

Leading a Church

- *Steadies.* There is a firmness to it even though it's constantly changing. Real vision includes core biblical truth, but the "how to" is flexible. Making disciples is the core. Where we do it, how we do it, and when we do it are aspects that may change.
- *Controls.* It beckons when all else is up for grabs. When everything around us is changing, vision reminds us of what matters most. Gifted leaders have the ability to focus on the vision and to bring all decisions back to it when necessary.
- *Empowers.* It first empowers your people and then the people you hope to reach. Vision causes your people to give their lives away in service to others, and it creates a radical difference in people's lives when they join with your church.
- *Honors.* Vision honors the past but prepares for the future. It does not trample on your history but instead radically moves your history into a more fruitful future.
- *Activates.* It lives in the now. It may be the big picture, but at some point vision must take on shoe leather. Vision that is never lived out is a daydream, not real vision.

Q: *Okay, I get it. So, how do I determine what the vision is for my church?*

A: Each pastor and church determines its vision in different ways, but the following are typical aspects of the process all churches appear to use.

- *Spend time with God.* We cannot develop vision without spending time with God. The key is prayer,

55

especially prayer that listens to what God says in his Word. Ask God to show you his dream for your ministry. It also means spending time in God's Word. Read and meditate on great passages of Scripture such as Matthew 28:19–20, Acts 2:37–47, and Ephesians 4:7–16.

- *Determine how God has uniquely gifted you for ministry.* God has uniquely created you with your desires, passions, interests, gifts, and talents. It is rare for God to ask us to lead a vision that does not fit us in some manner or form.
- *Find other visionary people.* Between 5 and 10 percent of every congregation are people of vision. Find these people in your own church and spend time with them contemplating God's Word, praying, and thinking about what God wants to accomplish through your church in the future.
- *Look at what God is blessing in your church.* Where does God appear to be working in your own church? God speaks through the gifts, talents, and passions of your people.
- *Uncover where God is working in your community.* God has placed your ministry in a particular context. The Holy Spirit is already there working, creating responsiveness, and opening doors of ministry. Find the open doors in the community. It is likely that God has provided resources through your people to meet needs in the community.
- *Dream.* If your church could be all God wants it to be in the next five years, what would it look like? Envision a picture of what the future might look like,

Leading a Church

then write it down. This is God's vision for your ministry. At first it might be a little blurry. That's okay. Just get started moving into the future. God will let you see the next steps on the journey as you move forward.

Q: *My church spent a lot of time developing a new vision, but it didn't seem to help. Why do you think that is?*

A: Much more than a vision is needed to set direction for a church. Establishing a new direction takes patience, tenacity, gentle persuasion, good communication, and, most of all, time. Here are a few insights:

- *You can't rent a vision.* Borrowing a vision statement from a successful church may seem like a good idea at first. However, it's akin to renting a car. While it's nice, it's not yours. You don't own it! Effective vision statements are owned by the congregation, not just rented.

- *Vision lacks clarity.* Even when vision is treated as significant, it assumes an undefined content to be filled in by the audience. Expressed differently, an illusion of communication is present in the word vision. When a person hears that word, they think they know what it means but rarely do. More problematic, each hearer fills in the content differently according to their own perceptions, assumptions, and biases.

- *A pastor must take responsibility for leadership.* In part this means creating clarity in a sea of confusion. It's best to assume that the board and other formal and informal church leaders don't know how to give or set direction. It's extremely rare to see a board or committee determine a church's vision. Thus, it falls to the pastor to nudge them along toward the future.

- *Setting direction is a process, not an event.* It takes more than a weekend retreat to establish a new direction for a local church. No one should attempt to set a new direction for a church unless they're willing to commit to a minimum of three years of hard work, sometimes longer.

- *You can't plan forever.* An old proverb says, "One who deliberates fully before taking a step will spend their entire life on one leg." An average plan put into action is better than an excellent plan left undone. The point is to get moving and let God direct your steps along the way (see Prov. 16:9).

Q: Do you have any tips for communicating a church's vision so that it's heard and accepted by the congregation?

A: Vision shapes the future from decade to decade, even century to century, but only when communicated well.

- *Communicate actively.* Important words call for actions. Use verbs and summon people to transformation. Use the positive voice rather than the negative.

- *Communicate repeatedly.* Vision becomes second nature to us, but our people forget it in two to four weeks.

- *Communicate memorably.* Use words and slogans that people will remember. Consider the power of Jesus's statement "I have come to seek and save the lost" (see Luke 19:10).

- *Communicate pictorially.* Use stories that illustrate the vision. Tell the same stories repeatedly until people identify the story with the vision.
- *Communicate excitedly.* Share your passion in everything you say and do. Talk about the future in all your meetings.

Design a Plan

Q: What place does planning have in church ministry?

A: Pastors and others occasionally resist the idea that churches should organize. Reasons churches give for not organizing vary, but in general they view management as unnecessary, uninteresting, unbiblical, and lacking trust in God.

A close look at the biblical record, however, demonstrates that God himself is a planner and organizer. He could even be called the premier organizer. The principles of organizing and organization are seen throughout Scripture. The following examples from the Old Testament show God's nature as a planner:

- The creation of the world (Gen. 1)
- Instructing Noah to build the ark (Gen. 6)
- Giving the Ten Commandments and the law (Exod. 20)
- Providing detailed plans for building the tabernacle and its furnishings (Exod. 25–30)
- Telling Joshua to send out the twelve spies (Josh. 2)
- Solomon's building the temple (1 Kings 6)
- Nebuchadnezzar's dream and Daniel's interpretation (Dan. 2:31–45)

The grandest example of planning is the birth of Christ as the fulfillment of God's plan of salvation (Matt. 1). Paul tells us that God has even created in advance all the good works we will do: "For we are His workmanship, created in Christ Jesus for good works, which God prepared beforehand so that we would walk in them" (Eph. 2:10 NASB). God truly does whatever he pleases in heaven and on earth, in the seas and all deeps (Ps. 135:6).

Years ago, Christians would often close their letters with "DV," which stands for the Latin phrase *Deo volente*, "if God wills" or "God willing." Any statements we make about tomorrow, next week, or next year are made in faith. Notice how our responsibility to plan is balanced with God's will in the following verses:

- "The plans of the heart belong to a person, but the answer of the tongue is from the LORD" (Prov. 16:1 NASB).
- "The mind of a person plans his way, but the LORD directs his steps" (Prov. 16:9 NASB).
- "Many plans are in a person's heart, but the counsel of the LORD will stand" (Prov. 19:21 NASB).

Plainly, planning in faith is biblical and an action that Christians are expected to practice, trusting in God to provide final confirmation and direction.

Q: My church needs lots of work. I get the idea of not making too many major changes the first year, but changes must be made. How do I know where to start? When and how should I begin?

Leading a Church

A: It's the rare church that doesn't need some changes. Like someone once said, "There are no perfect churches. If you find one, don't go there, as you'll make it imperfect." The first year is a good time to analyze the church. As you're building relationships, ask good questions to help you understand the background, current situation, and future needs of the church. I've found the following five questions reveal much helpful information. Don't ask them all at one time.

- What is working well at this church?
- What is not working well?
- What do I need to know to really understand this church?
- What stories, people, or events are legendary?
- If I could change one thing at this church, what would it be?

Q: *Listening to people is a good way to start, but when you boil it down, it's just their opinions. How can my analysis be more objective?*

A: When people share their thoughts, they of course may be correct or incorrect. One way to sift out incorrect feelings is to compare results to actual statistics. Here is a good plan to follow during the first year:

- Take time to look at the church's indicators of growth and decline. Begin by graphing the previous ten years of the church's worship attendance, membership, financial giving, number of adult baptisms and/or conversions to faith, number of people serving in a ministry (using their gifts), and number of those who actively participate in some discipleship activity. Healthy churches see about 62 percent growth in these areas over a decade (or 5 percent a year). Less than that indicates there are some areas of weakness.

- Analyze these six areas and compare them to the people's subjective input. This will help you reach a reasonable conclusion about what needs to be done in the coming years.
- Based on your findings, think through what needs to be addressed and design a simple plan to get started during your second year.

Communicate Well

Q: *Communication always seems to be difficult in a church. How can I do a better job at communicating to a varied audience?*

A: At first glance, it appears that communication in a church is easy. A look at the communication system, however, reveals that communication is complex. The average person in the United States receives between four thousand and ten thousand messages per day. But here's the shocking news: Of those messages, only about a hundred, or less than 2 percent, are remembered. Is it any wonder that people in our churches don't recall announcements from the pulpit or on the church website? Consider the following insights:

- A *church has multiple communication channels.* Some people will receive information via the grapevine, but others are outside that loop and never get the information as it's passed from person to person. They may get their information from looking at posted announcements on the church's website. If the website is not updated on a regular basis—say, weekly—they never receive the messages in a timely manner. Some listen for announcements during the church's worship service. Others gain information from communication channels such as social media, email, texts, newsletters, pastoral visits, lay visits, phone calls, or special mailings. At minimum, every church has thirty or more channels it uses to communicate with the congregation.

- *The grapevine is fast but not always accurate.* Someone hears something, then passes it along to another person, who in turn passes it along to still another person until numerous people have heard. In general, the larger the congregation and the more scattered the people are, the less accurate the communication that travels over the grapevine.
- *Some people will not get the message.* With so many communication channels available, it's best to assume that some people in the church will not receive messages. One-way communication that doesn't include the possibility of feedback is particularly vulnerable. An announcement is sent out, but there may be no way to know how many people receive the message.
- *Some people do not understand the message.* Some messages get garbled in transmission, while others may not be as clear as the sender intended them to be. This is particularly apparent when communication is delivered by social media. Messages sent

electronically are particularly prone to misinterpretation and misunderstanding.

- *Some people will not remember the message.* How quickly we forget. Even with the best intentions, received communication is laid aside, misplaced, or forgotten in today's busy world.
- *Some people receive a message that was never sent.* People tend to hear what they want to hear. Thus, even the clearest words are often misinterpreted by the listeners.
- *Silence does not mean acceptance.* Even though members of the congregation may hear and understand a communication correctly, it doesn't mean they agree with it. Too often the fact that people don't express disagreement is taken to mean they agree, which isn't true. Don't assume silence is agreement.
- *Two-way communication is better than one-way.* A person-to-person phone call is better communication than a one-way text. Any communication that allows for immediate feedback is best. Thus, person-to-person communication (e.g., a luncheon meeting) is better than object-to-person communication (e.g., an email).
- *The importance of a message is determined by the recipient.* Communication that begins with the recipient's interests, concerns, or problems in mind is more likely to be read and understood than one that begins with the sender's concerns.
- *Messages communicated multiple times and in multiple ways are best.* A good rule is to communicate all important messages five different ways. This doesn't mean sending out a message five times by email, for

Leading a Church

example, but rather sending it on five different channels of communication.

- *Different people require different channels of communication.* Channels that reach people in your congregation don't normally work to reach people outside of your church (churched vs. unchurched). Those that reach active members don't always reach inactive ones (churched vs. dropouts). Some channels are appropriate for some messages but not for others (members vs. nonmembers).

5

PASTORING A CHURCH

Preaching

Q: A pastor I admire says preaching is the key to leading a church well. What do you think?

A: There's no doubt that preaching is a major—maybe *the* major—element in fruitful church ministry. The apostle Paul told Timothy to "preach the word" (2 Tim. 4:2). So, what kind of preacher brings God to people and people to God? What kind of preacher creates an atmosphere where growth can occur?

- *A call from God*. Pastors of growing churches operate from a sense of call rather than a feeling of drivenness. They know they are stewards, not owners. Driven preachers act as though they own the people; called preachers act as stewards of the people. Paul encouraged Timothy to "fan into flame the gift of God" (2 Tim. 1:6). Pastors who desire to see their church growing must fan the flame of their calling to preach. God calls pastors in numerous ways, but every call to preach will have some combination of the following four aspects:

1. A sense in their spirit that God wants them to preach. It's a mission they can't give up.
2. An awareness of effectiveness when they preach. It's an aha experience that convinces them they were born to preach.
3. An affirmation from mentors and others around them. No one is called in a vacuum; all are called in a matrix of people, a congregation of like-minded others who affirm the gift of preaching.
4. A congruity of circumstances that opens doors of opportunity; for example, a spouse is willing to support you, a friend recommends you to a church, or a preaching ministry is available.

- *An attitude of authenticity.* Pastors of growing churches let the people see them as real human beings. What inspires people is not hearing about a pastor's knowledge or administrative skill or leadership ability; it's seeing them as people who struggle with life issues as all Christians do. People see the pastor as real, as authentic, when they are allowed to peek into their family, work, and spiritual life. One does not need to share intimate life details; a small peek goes a long way to inspire others and to let them know you struggle too.

- *A presentation of excellence.* Every craft or skill is backed up by practice. If you desire to play the piano, for example, you'll practice playing scales. Hours of playing scales makes the finger muscles limber and strong and creates muscle memory so playing piano pieces comes easily. What are the scales a pastor must practice to become a better preacher? First, you must preach. Take every opportunity to preach that you possibly can. Research has shown that it takes around five thousand hours of practice to become good at something. How many hours a week do you preach? How long will it take you to amass five thousand hours? Other scales include the spiritual scale (your quiet time); the intellectual scale (your reading time); the intercession scale (your prayer time); the relational scale (your people time); and the writing scale (your thinking time).
- *A clear message.* Evaluating a pastor's preaching can be difficult. A sermon is a creative act—a subjective thing. However, here are a few aspects to analyze for effective communication:
  - *Is it biblical?* The pastor is responsible for the content of the message. Make sure it flows out of Scripture and remains true to Scripture.
  - *Is it prepared?* For most pastors, developing a good message takes no less than fifteen hours a week. Are you putting in the time?
  - *Is it clear?* Does the message have a point? Do you restate the point at least three to five times throughout the sermon?

- *Is it illustrated well?* Stories engage people. Support each major point in your message with a story.
- *Is it action-oriented?* Give two ideas on what to do following the message.

Q: *Is it possible to improve my preaching?*

A: Yes, it is. And if you want your church to grow, you must improve. Good preaching, of course, depends on a number of factors.

- *Know your God.* Pastors have all been taught, in one way or another, techniques or processes for putting a sermon together. But finding a formula for experiencing the awe or special anointing or work of the Holy Spirit in a sermon is akin to trying to find the smell of a rose by pulling off each petal. There's a mysterious aspect that older pastors used to call unction. All pastors need some sort of process for putting together their sermons, but if a pastor doesn't know God personally and deeply, nothing is likely to happen.

- *Know yourself.* If we really know God, then we must consider ourselves in the light of his attributes. In doing so, we realize our personal failure to live up to God's standards and our own need of forgiveness and redemption. Thus, we come to the sermon *as one who needs the Savior.* The tone of our sermons inevitably reflects this knowledge, as we appropriately admit our own struggle with living the Christian life. The sermon then projects an air of authenticity rather than superiority. It communicates a feeling

Pastoring a Church

of humility rather than pride. It presents an aura of reality rather than pretense. We also must come to the sermon *as one who has the Savior*. Knowing ourselves means we not only know our weaknesses and failures, but we know the liberty, hope, and joy found from embracing the Savior's redemption. We can stand in the pulpit knowing our frailties and also the Savior's grace. Thus, we preach as *participants* in the message rather than *performers* of the message. Instead of hiding our weaknesses (performers), we allow our personalities to come out (participants), knowing that God applies his Word to human hearts through authentic messengers. It is a glorious thing to be yourself. Preaching really is delivering truth through personality.

- *Know your text.* Pastors typically don't find exegesis hard. They can work their way through the Scriptural text, get the flow of thought, and understand the context. They know the basics of sermon preparation: choose the text, determine what it means, meditate on it, isolate the dominant thought, arrange the material to serve the dominant thought, add the introduction and conclusion, and so forth. What's much more difficult, of course, is determining what a text means for today. Knowing the text implies both accurately exegeting it and also letting it touch your own life. Good preaching arises out of truly wrestling with the text—thinking about it and experiencing it in some fashion. How has it touched your own life? Where have you seen it worked out in others' lives? Knowing the text is a two-sided coin: Know what it meant to the original writer and know what it means to people today.

- *Know your audience.* The major league of preaching is seeing people change their lives to become more like Jesus. Be aware of the questions people are asking. Each generation asks different questions. Younger people in their twenties want to know where to center their lives—around God, work, or friends? Those in their thirties face serious responsibilities—mortgages, spouses, babies, in-law relationships, and work stressors. They have many questions revolving around these aspects of life. For people in their forties, they wonder about career and marriage disappointments. Should they scale back their dreams or forge ahead? By their fifties, people wonder if they're past their prime. Few friendships, children leaving the home, and less than satisfying jobs force unexpected feelings to the surface. Some fight feelings of loss, search for intimacy in wrong places, and wonder if they bring value to anyone any longer. Those in their sixties wonder what it means to be old, if they look as old as their peers, and how to deal with long-term resentments. For people in their seventies and beyond, questions arise as to how long they have left on this earth, how to maintain their independence as they grow older, and what will happen to the family when they're gone.

You must know the people to address these fears, inadequacies, and regrets. If you can't peer into their eyes and see their hurt and lostness, you have little right to preach the gospel to them. You must know some of them well enough to speak to their pains, struggles, and hopes. Let them see that you know and understand what they need to know and do to follow Christ in their world.

Caring for Others

Q: *This past week a church member talked to me in the parking lot. They were upset that I hadn't visited their mother in the nursing home every month. I know pastoral care is important to ministry, but I just don't have the time or energy to meet each member's expectations. What can I do?*

A: Church attendees today don't expect as much personal care from a pastor as they did in the past. As a pastor, however, you should cultivate a strategic presence. Here are some ideas on how to do so.

- *Be visible.* Some pastors hide out before, between, and after worship services. Being in the green room may be comfortable, but you'll have a more strategic presence if you walk through the lobby and take time to greet and speak with people. You don't need to engage in long conversations; just take time to speak with a few. Not everyone will get to talk with you, but everyone will know that you are there.
- *Talk, listen, and ask questions.* Focus on the person you're talking to and resist looking past them to the next person. Learn to say "I'm sorry," "I don't know," "I'm happy for you," "How can the church help?," "Will you forgive me?," and "I forgive you."
- *Thank people for their concern but don't promise results.* When people share a criticism, nicely explain

that you can't do anything about the issue. Encourage them to talk to the right person or department. If they share a need, point them to the right ministry or have them call the office and make an appointment to talk to you later. Resist the urge to jump right in to provide an answer or a solution in the moment.

- *Thank people for their service to Jesus and your church.* A few words of appreciation will empower most people for a long time. Small, handwritten notes carry powerful aromas of care in today's digital world.
- *Make strategic appearances.* Be present with people at key moments. Remember, funerals are mandatory; weddings are optional. Know your people and culture, and show up at key times.
- *Make pastoral phone calls.* Make one phone call a day to a randomly selected person who attends your church. Keep the conversation short, ask the person how they are doing, let them know you care about them, and thank them for being part of the church. Talk to whomever answers the phone. If it's a little child, teenager, or other family member, talk with that person.
- *Get out of the office.* Book at least one or two appointments a week with people to talk about real-world issues. Meet near places where people work. Don't talk about the church or church issues, but discuss life in the real world. Focus on what is pressing in on their lives. Ask what they cry about, what they rejoice about, their work, families, and friends.
- *Cautions:* When a church holds on to the practice of the pastor as the primary caregiver, it results in negative consequences.

- The quality and quantity of care is limited to the capacity of the pastor.
- A church is limited in its ability to grow and provide qualitative and quantitative care for the souls of people.
- Pastors do not have time to carry out their mission of equipping the saints for ministry (Eph. 4:11–12).
- It creates an unhealthy cycle of dependency and codependency between the pastor and the people of the church.
- Pastors do physical, spiritual, and emotional damage to themselves and their families.

Q: Helping people to walk through grief is a challenge for me. Can you give me some hints to help me better serve my people facing issues of loss?

A: Grief is a normal and natural response to loss. The loss may be of a loved one who died, a dream for the future, a beloved pet, a well-liked job, or a host of other life events that are devastating, frightening, and lonely. It is important to remember the following insights about grief:

- Grief is like a wound that heals but leaves a scar. Life will never be the same, but eventually a person will get better.
- Grief is a common experience, but no two people grieve the same.
- Grief feelings arise from deep within the individual. While feelings are neither right nor wrong, they may cause a person to say or do things that are uncharacteristic.

- Grief cannot be controlled; a person must go through it. Times of sorrow, rage, and despair are intermingled with times of peace, hope, and joy.
- Grief can be redeemed. A person can choose to accept or reject their feelings, to face them or deny them.
- Grief needs to be expressed. Find someone to listen and talk to them; share your feelings.
- Grief has no timetable. Take one hour and one day at a time. It takes longer than most people expect.
- Grief demands grief work. The work of grief is described as mourning. The four main tasks of mourning are:

  1. Accepting the reality of the loss
  2. Experiencing the pain of grief
  3. Adjusting to a world in which what was lost is missing
  4. Reinvesting energy in life and a new direction

Q: What steps can I take to help those experiencing grief?
A: The ability to help those who are grieving is a major aspect of caregiving. Here are some suggestions to get started:

- *Be supportive.* Visit or call to say "I care and want to help." Sit quietly with them as they mourn.
- *Treat each person equally.* Each person processes grief differently.
- *Be available.* Provide direct help by cooking, doing errands, making phone calls, cleaning the house, mowing a yard, or washing a car.

- *Allow people to express their grief.* Don't judge them for what they say or do during the grieving process.
- *Restate their expressed feelings.* Explain that it is okay to feel hurt and angry.
- *Ask how you can pray for them.* Then pray whatever they say.
- *Be careful what you say.*

  What to say:
  - "I'm sorry."
  - "I'm so sad for your loss."
  - "I know this must be terribly hard for you."
  - "How are you managing all of this?"
  - "What can I do for you?"
  - "I'm here and I want to listen."
  - "Talk as long as you wish. I have plenty of time."
  - "You don't have to say anything at all."

  What not to say:
  - "I understand."
  - "It's all happened for the best."
  - "This was God's way of saying something was wrong."
  - "You should feel lucky that . . ."
  - "Forget it. Put it behind you and get on with your life."
  - "You'll get over it."
  - "You're better off that this happened."[1]

---

1. Adapted from Catherine Lammert, "Counseling the Grief-Stricken," Christian Life Resources, accessed November 26, 2024, https://christianliferesources.com/2018/05/04/counseling-the-grief-stricken/.

Q: Is there a normal process for people going through grief?

A: There are two models of the grief process: the traditional model and the current model.

Grief Model #1: Traditional Grief Cycle

People who experience loss are plunged into a grief cycle. It is akin to riding a roller coaster as it goes up and down and around—sometimes even upside down. Unpredictable emotions can be embarrassing, disruptive, and frightening. The traditional grief cycle as proposed by Dr. Elisabeth Kübler-Ross has five stages:

- *Denial*: "This can't be happening to me." People deny that a loss is happening to them. Feelings such as anger, sadness, and hurt are not recognized or admitted.
- *Anger*: "Why is God allowing this to happen?" As people move out of denial, they become angry and cannot make sense of their loss. Some feel they are being unfairly treated by a boss or family member or even God. Their anger is often directed toward those who are closest to them, such as a spouse, parent, child, doctor, or themselves.
- *Bargaining*: "Please God, change this situation and I'll . . ." In desperation a person may plead with God to restore a loved one to health or give them back their career or fulfill their lost dream. They hope to convince God to reverse their loss in exchange for a payment of some sort.
- *Depression*: "I just want to die; I don't want to live any longer." When the loss is not reversed, deep

feelings of sadness and apathy may set into the person's life. They may sleep all night but wake up just as tired as when they went to bed. They may find it difficult to sleep at night, then all they want to do in the daytime is sleep. Some have crying spells, loss of appetite, decreased energy, and lose the will to engage life.

- *Acceptance*: "I accept the reality of my loss and am ready to move forward." A person accepts their loss and deals with the fears about the future. While they may continue to experience tinges of sadness from time to time, they are not overwhelmed with the loss and it doesn't preoccupy their life.

These five stages of the traditional grief cycle don't always happen in order. They may also be repeated more than once before acceptance is achieved. However, awareness of this cycle will help you understand others and make sense of the emotional chaos they experience.

Grief Model #2: Current Grief Cycle

Grief is not something to be fixed; it is something to go through. It is comparable to a bomb that is dropped unexpectedly into a person's life.

Stage 1: Impact

When the bomb of loss is dropped, a person is dazed and shocked. Their heart rate goes up and they panic as adrenaline flows through their body. Eating patterns change, and they either sleep a lot or can't sleep at all. This stage lasts from one to two months, and a church family best supports the person experiencing the loss by providing prayer and care for physical needs such as meals.

Stage 2: Fallout

Following the initial shock, a person experiences a time of fallout. They become tired and depressed, with bouts of sadness and joy, ups and downs for three to four months. As they survey the damage to their life, they ask questions like "Why me?" and "Where's God?" A church family best supports the grieving person by visiting and taking time to listen.

Stage 3: Wandering

As a person processes their loss, they gradually discover a new stabilized life. While they occasionally slip backward in their grief work, they slowly emerge with a new story of hope for the future in six to twelve months. A church best supports them with occasional visits to check on their health, provide biblical teaching, and answer questions.

Stage 4: Rebuilding

The rebuilding stage takes place in months thirteen to eighteen, as the person experiences regular life patterns once again. A church best supports them by helping them chart a fresh beginning for their life.[2]

Officiate Weddings

Q: I've been asked to officiate a wedding. Are there essential guidelines that are good to keep in mind?

2. This content is adapted from Jason Cusick, 5 *Things Any Congregation Can Do to Care for Others* (Wesleyan Publishing House, 2009), 12–16. Used by permission.

A: It's an honor to officiate a wedding, but before you even consider the opportunity, it's wise for a church to establish a wedding policy. A wise wedding policy will guide you in determining which weddings you may officiate, while protecting you from difficult situations. Policies often cover:

- Use of facilities
- Divorce and remarriage
- Premarital counseling
- Who may officiate weddings

As the officiating pastor, make certain all requirements are met for the state in which you reside. It is normal that you be ordained or licensed to conduct weddings. However, some states allow others to officiate if they've completed the proper paperwork.

It's best to require premarital counseling for couples who ask you to marry them. Much time and money are spent on the wedding ceremony and reception, which lasts only a few hours, but little time and money are spent on preparing for a lifetime of marriage. An investment in premarital counseling is wise. If you are unsure whether you want to officiate a wedding, agree to do the premarital counseling but defer your decision to officiate until after the sessions have concluded.

There are many ways to organize a wedding service. Obtain and use a minister's service manual. Each denomination usually has their own, but there are several good ones available for pastors leading nondenominational churches. It's also a good idea to use a standard book on wedding etiquette, as they offer suggestions on how to work with difficult situations such as the seating arrangement of divorced parents.

The Pastor

- Design the order of service with the bride and groom prior to the ceremony.
- Rehearse the ceremony with everyone present who will be a part of the wedding.
- Practice everything in the rehearsal that will happen in the wedding ceremony.
- Examine the marriage license and check the date; make sure it hasn't expired. You may only conduct a wedding with a valid license from the state in which the marriage takes place.
- Obtain all signatures on the license.
- Make a photocopy of the license for your files and the church's records.
- Mail the completed license to the county clerk following the wedding.
- Keep your own personal record and remember each anniversary.

Ceremony Order

The following is a traditional Western Protestant wedding ceremony. Elements may be altered or deleted or added. The meaning and symbolization of the elements could be understood in different ways.

- Guests and parents seated
- Lighting of candles
- Music
- Groomsmen enter
- Bridesmaids and maid-of-honor enter

- Bride and father enter (mother previously seated)
- Opening remarks/prayer
- Exchange of bride's hand
- Bride and groom walk to places
- Declaration of intent
- Short prayer and/or music
- Charge to bride and groom
- Prayer of commitment
- Music
- Wedding vows
- Ring exchange
- Pronouncement of husband and wife
- Lighting of unity candle or taking communion
- Kiss
- Presentation (using new names)
- Recessional
- Dismissal of congregation
- Reception line

Hospital Visitation

Q: What are some guidelines for visiting people in the hospital? I know it's a key time to minister, but I honestly don't feel comfortable in a hospital setting.

A: All Christians are responsible for visiting the sick (see Matt. 25:36; James 1:27), but doing so is an especially important aspect of ministry for pastors and elders (see James 5:12–18). Involving members in hospital visitation isn't easy, but it's worth the effort and time to build a solid visitation plan.

Train Your People

- Teach that it is the responsibility of the sick person or their family to call for a pastoral visit. People do not expect a physician to initiate a visit; they must not expect the pastor to do so either.
- Teach that you are neither omniscient nor omnipresent, and that in our fast-paced society the news that someone is hospitalized is not always received. People should not assume that the pastor or other elders know someone is sick.
- Teach that the sick person or their family should call for the pastor when they're ready.
- Teach that a visit to the sick is not merely to hold their hand and pray but an opportunity for ministry to wider aspects of their lives.
- Train your people to care for one another.

Plan for the Visit

- Find out why the person is in the hospital.
- Find out how serious their condition is, as this determines the urgency of the visit.
- Determine the appropriate length of the visit and select a Scripture passage to read. Do not simply read the Scripture but explain and apply it. Some appropriate texts include:

  Job 1:20–22; 2:7–10; 42:10, 12

  Psalms 32; 38; 51; 77; 107:17–22; 119:50, 52, 67, 71, 75, 92

  Romans 8:18–39

1 Corinthians 15:51–58

2 Corinthians 1:3–7

Hebrews 2:14–15; 4:15–16

James 1:2–4; 5:11, 13–16

When to Visit

- As soon as possible.
- Visit before the person enters the hospital and/or before the operation.
- Visit following the operation as soon as healing permits.
- Do not visit at the hospital in the morning, which is often the busiest time for doctors, hospital staff, and patients.
- Find out your local hospital's clergy visitation policy by calling and asking.
- If possible, visit outside of posted visiting hours to avoid interrupting other visitors.

At the Hospital

- Present yourself as a pastor or clergy at the information, emergency, or nurses' desk.
- Introduce yourself and inquire about information on the patient to help you determine the time and length of your visit. Do not ask, "What is Mr. Jones's condition?" Instead say something like, "I do not want to overly tire Mr. Jones. Can you give me some indication of the severity of his condition?"
- If the person is sleeping, it may not be wise to wake them. Instead, leave a note or card to let them know

you stopped by. Or ask at the nurses' station to see what they would recommend.

- If the room door is closed, knock before entering or check at the nurses' station first so you do not embarrass the person.

Length of Your Visit

- Stay no longer than is necessary.
- Stay no longer than the patient can endure. The standing rule is that the more serious the patient's condition, the shorter and more frequent your visits should be.
- In nearly all situations it is best to err on the side of brevity.
- Ask the patient to tell you when they are tired.

During the Visit

- Listen to the patient.
- Read a short passage of Scripture.
- Pray with the patient. [Note: Ask the patient what they would like you to pray about. Then pray what they mention.]
- Some don'ts:
  - Do not sit on the bed. In a real sense, the bed is the one personal piece of property possessed by the patient in the hospital and must not be invaded.
  - Do not say things that are not true.
  - Do not overstay your visit.

Pastoring a Church

- Do not forget to minister to others who are present. Serious illness usually affects more people than the one who is sick.
- If the patient is in a coma, remember he or she may still be able to hear. Hearing is the last of our senses to fade. Thus, be careful what you say to others in earshot of the patient. Speak and pray with the patient as though they can hear you. Assume they can, and speak words of comfort directly to them.

Visiting a Contagious Person

- Visit by phone or video call if possible.
- Ask the hospital for assistance. They will provide special garments (e.g., mask, gown, shoe covers).
- Make the visit as brief as possible.
- Do not touch the sick person, the bed, or anything else in the room.
- Wash your hands and face as soon as possible upon leaving the room. Do not wait until you get home; use the washroom in the hospital.

Visiting the Dying

- Try to speak with the patient alone.
- Never say you know the person is dying. God is ultimately in control of death, and he may prolong life.
- Deal with the patient as if death were a distinct possibility. Death always changes the conversation.
- Speak directly about death and eternal life. Death changes the calculations. Things that seemed

important in life no longer hold sway. Speak words that are deep, clear, and true.

- Present the simple facts of the gospel. The theme of all conversation with the dying should be the plan of salvation.
- Ask the person if they know Christ as their Savior. If not, ask them if they would like to pray to receive Christ.
- If the person does know Christ, reassure them of the hope they have in him.
- Share a brief Scripture—one or two verses is enough —and pray with them. Here are a few suitable passages you could read: John 3:16; 3:36; 5:24; 14:1–8; Psalms 23; 90.

Dos and Don'ts of Hospital Visits

- Do wash your hands before leaving the hospital.
- Don't pump the person for information about their condition.
- Do be sensitive as to the length of the visit (depends on the situation).
- Don't sit on the patient's bed, even if they say it's okay.
- Do help the person get the information they need from staff.
- Don't wear heavy perfume or cologne.
- Do honor the person's physical space and informational privacy.
- Don't provide physical assistance without asking nursing staff to help as needed.

- Do be careful around the medical equipment and watch so you don't step on tubes and other items.

Conduct Funerals

Q: There's been a death in one of my church families and I've been asked to preside over the funeral. Any suggestions?

A: At no time is there a greater call for the pastor's sympathetic and spiritual service than at the time of a death. The pastor needs to pray for a special preparation of heart for this ministry. At such a time he may have a spiritual influence that will never be forgotten, or he may do untold injury to the cause of Christ by neglect or carelessness.

Teaching About Death and Dying

Teaching people about death and dying is a crucial part of pastoral care. The following is a simple outline to use in such training.

- People handle death and dying in three ways:
  1. Denial—"I'm not going to die" (Mark 8:31–33).
  2. Deafness—"I don't want to talk about it"; "I don't want to hear about it or deal with it" (Mark 9:31–32).
  3. Dread—"I know what's coming and I'm afraid" (Mark 10:32–34).
- In John 11, we see Jesus handled death and dying in three ways:
  1. Hope (vv. 21–23)
  2. Assurance (vv. 24–29)
  3. Comfort (vv. 33–38)

Ministry in the Home Immediately Following a Death

- Make a visit as soon as news of the death is received. This visit may be brief. Express your sympathy. Let the family know that you are vitally concerned and ready to be of any service possible to them.
- Do not suggest the matter of funeral arrangements at this early date unless the family brings it up.
- Present some Christian truth, such as their loved one is in the presence of the Lord, the fact of reunion, the comforting presence of the Holy Spirit, or the sufficiency of God's grace.
- Be prepared for various situations you may encounter, such as those who have a rebellious spirit, those who feel that the loved one was not prepared to die, difficult family dynamics, or those who may be overmedicated.
- Offer reasonable assistance in any way possible, such as making a phone call or sending an email or text on the family's behalf. Be sincere in this offer.

Preparations for the Funeral

Often this matter is addressed during the pastor's second visit, after the family has had time to compose themselves a bit and think about what they want to do. There are instances where such preparation is all cared for in connection with the minister's first visit, but usually that is too soon for final arrangements to be made.

- Learn the desires of the family and comply with them as far as possible. Little things mean a lot at a time like this. Find out:

- Where will the funeral be held?
- Who will assist and how?
- Will there be an obituary? If so, who will write it?
- Will the service include music? Who will sing and/or play instruments? What hymns or songs will be included?
- What time is the service?
- Will there be a preliminary service with the family?
- Will the body lie in repose at the funeral home?
- Will the casket be open or closed?
- What are the appropriate customs?

Arrival at the Funeral Home

- Arrive at the funeral home at least fifteen minutes early.
- Notify the funeral director of your arrival; they will give you a copy of the obituary and any honorarium.
- Give the funeral director an order of service and go over it with them.
- If possible, meet with the family before the service and pray with them.

The Order of Service

The funeral service should be carefully planned so that it will not occupy more time than culturally appropriate. The effectiveness of a service is not determined by its length. Here is a sample order of service:

- Song
- Scripture reading

- Obituary
- Prayer
- Message
- Prayer
- Song

The Funeral Message

- Not too long (cultural situations vary).
- Emphasize the God of hope and mercy.
- Not too flowery. Be truthful.
- Characterized by tenderness and compassion. Remember how Jesus wept in connection with the death of Lazarus!

The Closing of the Service

- As soon as the service is completed, the funeral director takes charge.
- Stand at the head of the casket as people pass by to view the body.
- Remain close to the family as they say their final goodbyes to their loved one. Give words of comfort if appropriate.
- Stay with the casket as it's taken in procession to the funeral car.
- Stand to the side while the casket is being placed in funeral car.
- Go to your own car if you are driving to the gravesite.

The Service at the Grave

- *Funeral procession*: The order of cars in the procession to the cemetery is as follows: funeral car, family car(s), minister's car, others' cars.

- *Arrival at the cemetery*: Upon arrival at the cemetery, the pastor will go at once to the rear of the funeral car and await the removal of the casket, which he will precede to the grave usually accompanied by a cemetery attendant. Following the service, the pastor stands at the head of the casket while people proceed by.

- *Arrival at the grave*: Upon reaching the grave the pastor will go immediately to the foot of the grave where he conducts the committal service. Sometimes it is arranged for him to stand at the head of the grave. From this point the pastor conducts the committal and concludes with the benediction.

- *Committal forms*: Various forms are available, but it seems best to use Scripture itself for this service. I offer the following suggestions:

  - *At the grave of a believer*, read John 11:20–27 and say: "It is with confident hope and faith in Christ, the living Son of God, that we lay away the body of this brother (sister), looking forward to the morning of the resurrection when he (she) together with all the saints of God shall be clothed upon with the house which is from heaven, and shall be forever like him who has loved us and given himself for us. Until that morning we commit the body to its rest."

  - *At the grave of an unbeliever*, read Psalm 103:15–17 and say: "Here we lay to rest the body of our departed friend. His (her) spirit we leave in the hands of a just and compassionate God who doeth always that which is right. Inasmuch as this is the lot of all of us who are yet living, if the Lord delays his coming, let us determine 'to number our days that we may apply our hearts unto wisdom.' Let us dedicate ourselves fully to the resurrection and the life. 'He that believeth in me, though he were dead, yet shall he live: and whosoever liveth and believeth in me shall never die.'"

- *Prayer and benediction*: When the public service at the grave is finished, if possible, offer a private word of comfort to the bereaved.

Visit After the Funeral

The days and weeks after the funeral are a very lonely time for the bereaved. A call in the home in the few weeks following a funeral may provide a fruitful time of ministry.

Funeral Dos and Don'ts

- Do attempt to connect with the person before death occurs.
- Do listen well; be slow to offer advice.
- Do observe family dynamics, but don't attempt to fix.
- Do get the names right! Clarify pronunciations.
- Do get the biography or obituary early.
- Do handle the honorarium wisely; the gospel is at stake.
- Do dress appropriately (know the culture and ask if you don't).

- Do get to the service early.
- Do introduce yourself to the funeral director.
- Do speak to the congregants on behalf of the family and then to the family on behalf of the congregants.
- Don't miss the importance of the ceremonial role of pastor.
- Don't force the family to do what you want; rather, guide them with options.
- Don't pretend you know the deceased if you didn't.
- Don't ignore major issues in the deceased's life, but be gracious. Not everything has to be said or revealed.
- Don't be late.
- Don't be afraid of appropriate humor, but be discerning.
- Don't shake hands as people file by the casket (unless they initiate it).
- Don't step on the grave markers.
- Don't be vague at the conclusion of the service. Be direct: "This concludes the service."
- Don't leave immediately after the service is over. Transition away at an appropriate time.
- Don't neglect to give yourself time to grieve.

Sample Funeral Sermon

On the day of a funeral service, a funeral home prints a booklet with information about the deceased, the name of the person leading the service, and other basic details that attendees wish to know. Perhaps 75 to 85 percent of the time,

Psalm 23 is printed on the booklet, which makes it a delightful passage to use for a sermon. Below is a simple sermon outline based on this psalm, but you'll need to make it your own by adding details.

Theme: Jesus Christ Is Our Guide

- He's a guide down the good roads of life (vv. 1–3).
  - Green pastures: Blessings
  - Quiet waters: Rest and peace
  - Restores my soul: Strength and renewal
- He's a guide down the bad (or difficult) roads of life (vv. 4–5).
  - Death: As the resurrected Savior, he's qualified to guide us.
  - Enemies: As the loving Savior, he's qualified to comfort us.
- He's a guide down the eternal road of life (v. 6).
  - Dwell in the house of the Lord forever.
  - Can you say "the Lord is *my* shepherd"?

6

GROWING A CHURCH

Trigger Points

Q: *Churches need to grow, but I have limited time to invest. What areas are the most fruitful for reaching people?*

A: There is no guarantee that a church will grow. However, we can develop positive ministry habits that may eventually result in healthy church growth. Focusing on the right ministry habits brings growth because each one acts as a "trigger point," that is, a powerful action that brings results.

Here are seven trigger points that have been found to be the most important for church growth.

1. *Outreach.* Reaching and winning new people to Christ is the first action that brings growth to a local church. Unless a church finds a way to effectively share the gospel with new people, there is little chance for long-term growth.

2. *Assimilation.* After a church learns to reach new people for Christ, the next action that brings

growth is finding ways to help newcomers connect with the church family. If a church cannot discover ways to assimilate new people, there will be little fruit that remains.

3. *Leadership development.* Recruiting, training, and releasing new leaders must happen if ministry is to expand. It takes new ministries to reach new people, and new ministries are most often empowered by new leaders.

4. *Worship.* Few churches can grow without an inspiring worship service. Designing a worship service that engages the minds, hearts, and emotions of worshipers is clearly needed if a church is to grow.

5. *Preaching.* A recent study found that 91 percent of people who have attended church for less than two years rate the pastor's preaching as extremely important.[1] The main factor that kept these new people in the church was preaching that applied the Word of God to life.

6. *Spiritual development.* People in growing churches sense that they are maturing in their faith. They sense that their participation in the life of the church has a positive effect on their lives. The basic principle is "Growing people grow churches."

7. *Loving care.* Growing churches provide pastoral care for each member. But it is not the pastors who provide the care; rather, the people give pastoral care to one another, usually through small groups and classes.

1. Gary L. McIntosh, *Growing God's Church* (Baker Books, 2016), 148.

Leading a Growing Church

Q: The church I pastor is growing. How do I keep up?

A: Leading a growing church is challenging for many reasons. A major one is the reality that a pastor must change roles as the church becomes larger. The problem is twofold.

First, many pastors do not realize they must change roles as the church grows larger. For example, smaller churches need a pastor who operates in the relational role of a caregiver. They are viewed as everyone's friend who of course knows everyone by name. As a church becomes medium-sized, the pastor's role must change to that of an administrator who takes care of the newly enlarged program. When a church becomes even larger, the pastor again must change roles to that of a leader who casts vision for the future while managing an ever-growing staff and complex ministry. Churches often have the potential to grow larger; however, the pastor keeps the church artificially small due to either a lack of knowledge on how to change or a lack of willingness to change roles.

Second, smaller congregations usually resist the change in a pastor's role. They often interpret such a change as the pastor abandoning them. For example, in a smaller church a pastor might maintain an open-study policy. Members of the congregation are encouraged to drop by the pastor's office whenever they desire to talk or go to coffee. Then, as a church grows to medium-size, the pastor may change to a by-appointment-only policy in an effort to control the demands on their time. People who have previously been able to walk into the pastor's office at any time are offended by having to make an appointment.

A Process for Role Change

- Prioritize the use of time. As a church grows from small to medium-sized to large, a pastor must take better control of his time. To get things done this means he will have to set boundaries, such as having posted office hours, limiting time for counseling, and protecting time for study.

- Educate the congregation on the pastor's changing role so that the people will gain understanding. Clearly communicating to people about why the pastor cannot be as available as he was in the past is crucial. This fact has to be shared in multiple ways through sermons, private conversations, small gatherings, and so forth. As an example, I recall hearing one pastor say to the congregation from the pulpit, "You may be thinking 'Isn't it the pastor's job to visit us in the hospital?' Folks, it's just not possible. The church is too large for me to care for everyone." The pastor said this over and over through many different means until the people began to understand.

- Replace the pastor with other leaders who are visible to the people in the congregation. People don't like the idea of not seeing the main leader. As a lead pastor changes roles, the people must see other credible leaders become more visible so they can get a meaningful audience with a person in authority if needed. This is a fact that pastors often overlook when seeking to change roles. Note the pattern found in Exodus 18:13–27 as an example of how to go about doing this:

Step #1: Identify and clarify the problem (vv. 13–18). Moses judged the people from morning to evening. He was the visible leader that everyone wanted to talk to about their specific problems. However, the work was overwhelming and people became frustrated. The problem was identified and clarified, and Moses realized he was doing too much.

Step #2: Ask others for help (v. 14). It took another person to point out the problem and solution to Moses. Jethro began by asking questions (What are you doing? Why do you alone sit as judge?) to gain perspective and involve Moses in the process of problem identification. Note the major problem was that Moses viewed himself as indispensable.

Step #3: Outline a solution and plan (vv. 19–27). Moses found the answer was to replace himself with credible leaders who were available to the people.

- He determined his own priorities: "You be the people's representative before God" (v. 19).
- He established recruiting criteria—namely, trustworthy men who feared God and hated dishonest gain (v. 21).
- He trained them. He taught them the decrees and laws and showed them the way to live and the duties they were to perform (v. 20).
- He communicated the organizational structure: thousands, hundreds, fifties, and tens (v. 21).

- He communicated their level of authority. The difficult cases they brought to Moses, but the simple ones they decided themselves (v. 22).

Some of the keys to the growth and maturity of the nation of Israel as illustrated in this passage were God's favor on the people, the leader's recognition of his inability to do all the work, and the leader's willingness to recruit, train, and deploy a workforce that could meet the needs of the people. In a similar way, for lead pastors to change roles as a church grows larger, they must recognize God's favor found in the growth of his church, accept their own inability to do everything, and empower other leaders to take proper responsibility.

Factors of Growing Churches

Q: *Every church grows by growth factors or principles. What are the main ones I should know?*

A: The growth of any church is a combination of three factors: *spiritual*, *institutional*, and *contextual*.

Spiritual factors include prayer, fasting, holy living, obedience to God's Word, unity of the church body, reliance on the Holy Spirit, love for one another, and a host of other things related to the work of God in a local church. To assess the spiritual factors in your church, look for answers to the following questions:

- How active are church attendees in personal prayer?
- Does your church have regularly scheduled times of congregational prayer? If so, how many? How well attended are they?

- How involved are church leaders in prayer activities? Do leaders model prayer to the congregation?
- Does your church sponsor prayer retreats or other activities for focused prayer?
- Do staff members have organized prayer teams?
- How unified is the congregation?
- Are there any corporate sins that have not been addressed?
- How loving is your congregation?
- Are members involved with fasting?
- Is there a prayer chain ministry in the church?

Institutional factors include budgets, facilities, worship styles, seating and parking capacity, approaches to decision-making, plans (or lack thereof), and many more things related to the work of ministry. To assess the institutional factors in your church, look for answers to the following questions:

- What is the age of your church?
- Do you have adequate seating, parking, and space for children?
- How balanced are the different age groups?
- What is your church's growth history over the last decade? Growing? Plateaued? Declining?
- How long has your church been in existence? Is it new, young, mature, or aging in its life cycle?
- What percentage of your people are serving in an identifiable ministry?
- How many of your church's programs or ministries are focused inward on the existing body versus outward on the unreached in your community?

- What percentage of worshipers also participate in Sunday school or small groups?
- What is the average age of your congregation's attendees?
- What is your average worship attendance?

Contextual factors include the people in the church, neighborhood, and surrounding community, economic trends, architecture of the church building, and the language spoken at the church. To assess the contextual factors in your church, look for answers to the following questions:

- What is your church's geographical ministry area? How far will 90 percent of your people drive to church?
- Is your ministry area growing, plateaued, or declining? How does this impact your church?
- What is the socioeconomic makeup of the people in your community? Do your church attendees mirror that?
- What are the top five music styles among people in your community? Does your church reflect these in worship services?
- What is the ethnic makeup of people in your community? Is this reflected in your congregation?
- What are the needs of people in your community? Is your church speaking to any of these needs?
- Does your community have a clear architectural appearance? If so, does your church facility fit the style?
- What is the average educational level of people in your community? Are your church attendees above, below, or the same?

- What is the primary language spoken in your community? Do you use that language in your church services and ministries?
- What opportunities are there for your church to serve your community?

Insights

- All three factors are interrelated. Thus, the growth or lack of growth in a local congregation is quite complex.
- Dynamic churches work to understand and improve in all three areas rather than just one or two.
- The easiest factors to assess are institutional. They are the tangible elements related to growth.
- The most difficult factors to assess are contextual and spiritual. They are intangible elements related to growth.
- The most thorough assessment often comes through the involvement of an outside consultant or coach. As someone once noted, "It's difficult for fish to study water." Likewise, it's often difficult for those involved in a church to seriously assess their own church.

Train for Outreach

Q: My church hasn't seen many adults accept Christ in the last few years. What is a good way to begin creating a culture of outreach?

A: Encouraging and equipping people to connect with non-churched friends and relatives is the beginning of an effective evangelistic outreach in a church.

Churches that successfully reach new people for Christ focus on training a minimum of 10 percent of their people each year in friendship evangelism. It takes time to build the evangelistic consciousness of a congregation. This is particularly true when a church has seen little or no conversion growth for several years. While church leaders may desire to train many people quickly, the fact is that in most churches people are often not ready to participate in a new evangelistic program. Therefore, begin slowly by focusing on 10 percent of the adults. This represents the approximate number who will be open to nurturing more meaningful relationships with their non-Christian friends and relatives. By starting with this receptive 10 percent, your evangelistic emphasis will get off to a good start. The next year, other adults will have heard about the good experiences from the first year's training and be open to taking part.

In the second year, invite newcomers to join in the training. New members and new believers tend to have more unchurched contacts than do longtime members. Newcomers also have an initial excitement about the church and want to spread the word in any way possible. By recruiting and training newer people, you will see the evangelistic outreach of your church grow quickly.

Once a church has annually trained 10 percent of its adult members for five years, it reaches a turning point when half of the congregation has completed the training. A new attitude and sensitivity toward newcomers becomes evident throughout the congregation. And as a church continues to train 10 percent per year, dramatic new life and enthusiasm take root as a growing majority of members become interested in reaching new people for Jesus. Many good books and study guides are available for evangelism training. I recommend keeping the course active as a regular part of the educational process in your church. And don't forget to include it in new member classes.

There are two important things to consider as you plan your evangelism training.

First, realize that there is much baggage out there about the "e-word." Somehow along the way, the word "evangelism" came to be associated with knocking on strangers' doors, passing out tracts on street corners, and generally participating in activities that induce sweaty palms, stomach butterflies, and too-tight collars. So, if you expect to have people in your church sign up for evangelism training, recognize there are many misconceptions.

Second, realize that the traditional methods that many of us have been trained in for "doing evangelism" are not necessarily the only ways—or even the best ways—to participate in the process of making disciples. Three traditional approaches typically include (1) teacher to student, (2) salesperson to customer, and (3) friend to friend.

Which of these three approaches do you think comes to mind for most people when they hear the word "evangelism"? If you said the second one, you're right. However, research indicates that 81 percent of people who make a decision for Christ from the "salesperson to customer" evangelistic approach drop out of church involvement within a year. Another interesting but not surprising result from the research indicates that the third approach is by far the most effective in making disciples—that is, new believers and active members of a local church. Of those who make a commitment to Christ through this approach, 78 percent stay active and involved.[2]

So, the approach to the process of disciple-making is important, but obviously the content is too. Here are four simple yet profound questions that your evangelism training should help church members to answer:

1. How has being a Christian made a difference in my life?
2. What does it mean to be a Christian (in words understandable to a non-Christian)?
3. Why would I like my friend to be a Christian and a member of my church?
4. How does a person become a Christian (in understandable words)?

Take several weeks in your training to discuss, research, share, role-play, and reflect upon each question. When your people feel comfortable with their answers, they will be better equipped to share their faith in a natural, "friend to friend" manner.

Know Your Community

Q: I've read that the context of a local church has considerable impact on the church's growth potential. Is that true? If so, how do I get to know my community?

A: "Everyone Welcome" is often displayed on church signs. However, churches that try to reach everyone quite often end

2. Flavil Yeakley, "Research and the Growing Church," *Church Growth America* 7, no. 1 (1989): 4.

up reaching no one—or at least very few people—for Christ. In contrast, churches that are effectively reaching people for Christ have a well-defined target group.

Churches make well-intentioned mistakes that keep them from experiencing biblical church growth, and one of the major mistakes is to not do adequate research to understand the people they are seeking to reach with the gospel. Despite our good intentions, if the method of evangelism we use does not fit the particular harvest field, we will be ineffective. While reaching the whole world with the gospel is the mission of the Christian faith, fruitful churches recognize that the world is made up of many different audiences. Since different people groups have different cultures, needs, and methods of communication, a church that intentionally focuses to reach a specific group with the message of Christ will normally be much more effective than a church that tries to reach everyone with a general attempt.

Every church should have a sign that says "Everyone Welcome," but a deliberate strategy must be in place or they will only see accidental growth. At first glance, it may seem that aiming at select groups of people is not biblical. On further reflection, however, it becomes obvious that it is the only strategic way to actually reach the world for Christ. Think for a moment how God began to redeem the world. From the beginning, God has been concerned for the entire world, not just certain people. God's desire is to redeem every tribe, nation, people, and family upon the face of the earth. Yet, how did he go about reaching the world? His plan started with a clearly defined target audience in the person and family of Abram and worked outward from there to the whole world. Jesus also loved the entire world, but he began with a target group of Galileans and worked from there to reach the world.[3]

Your particular mission and vision, if it is to be fully realized, must be intentional. The question "For whom are we burdened?" does not arise out of selfish desires but out of a humble desire to come alongside particular peoples as missionaries, to identify with their pain and misfortune, and to lay down our lives for their welfare and for matters that impact their eternal destiny. Below are some ideas to help you find your specific target audience.

1. *Know yourself and your congregation.* Ask yourself questions such as: How old am I? What is the average age of people in my congregation? What do I like to read? What are people in my congregation reading? What music do I enjoy? What music do my people prefer? What is my educational level? What is the educational level of my congregation? Who tends to follow my leadership? After you answer these questions, make a list of people who may be a close match. If God directs your heart toward those who are different from you and your congregation, be willing to invest time in learning about them (e.g., language, values, communication, decision-making methods).

2. *Investigate the people and places you have listed as a potential target audience.* Where do people live who are similar to you? Once you have located where people live, begin to study them to determine their needs, struggles,

---

3. Adapted from Gary McIntosh, "Who Is Your Target Audience?," *The Good Book Blog*, October 12, 2012, https://www.biola.edu/blogs/good-book-blog/2012/who-is-your-target-audience.

and pains. Be sensitive to God's leading as you investigate the various groups of people in your community. To whom are you drawn? Which group of people has needs that your church is ready and able to meet?

3. *Look for those who are receptive and open to the gospel.* In general, people tend to be most receptive when they are going through changes, relocating, facing challenging circumstances, or when they have major needs. Which people that you have identified appear to be the most receptive?

4. *Narrow down your list to one or two groups of people.* Conduct additional research on the people God has placed on your heart and ask, To whom am I being drawn? Where am I most likely to be fruitful?

5. *Design a new ministry specifically aimed to meet a need of your target group.* Initiate it and begin working to reach this group for Christ and your church. Church leaders can no longer be inhibited about developing strategies aimed toward particular groups of people. Congregations that take the Great Commission seriously are burdened and drawn toward particular groups in their community and around the world.

Open Side Doors[4]

Q: The current ministries in my church aren't reaching new people. What can I do?

A: The front doors of America's churches are closing. Your church's "front doors" are your worship service, education

---

4. The content under this heading is adapted from Gary L. McIntosh and Charles Arn, *What Every Pastor Should Know* (Baker Books, 2013), 22–24.

classes, or special events. They are the primary way that most churches identify their prospective members. However, as the number of visitors has been declining, the front doors are not working as well. To survive, let alone to thrive, a church needs to build "side doors" to create connections with the people in their community who will find faith.

Q: What are side doors?

A: A side door is a church-sponsored program, group, or activity in which a nonmember can become comfortably involved on a regular basis. It is an ongoing function in which a nonmember can develop meaningful and valued relationships with people in the church. The purpose of a side door is to provide an opportunity for these group participants (both church members and nonmembers) to develop friendships around something important they share. And, as we now know, relationships are the key to effective evangelism. It is through relationships that the gospel has primarily spread throughout the centuries, as well as today.

Below are just a few examples of actual side doors that churches have created where members and nonmembers can develop friendships around common interests or seasons of life. There are side doors in churches for people who:

- ride motorcycles
- have children in the military
- own RVs
- are recent widowers
- are newlyweds
- enjoy reading books

- are unemployed
- suffer from chronic pain
- have spouses who are incarcerated
- have spouses who are not believers
- are fishing enthusiasts
- are single parents
- want to get in better physical condition
- want to help homeless families
- play softball
- are interested in end times
- serve as caregivers for aging parents
- are raising grandchildren
- are moms with teenage daughters

Q: *Why are side doors necessary today for churches to effectively reach out and evangelize?*

A: The longer a person has been a Christian, the fewer friends they have who are not Christians. Eventually, many longtime Christians have no real friends outside their church or faith. As a result, the outreach potential (and thus the growth potential) of a church that consists of mostly longtime Christians is quite limited compared to a church with many new believers. If your church is made up mostly of people who have been Christians for over five years, you need to build at least two side doors each year where people can develop new friendships with those outside the church.

Q: *How does a church begin creating side doors—new groups, new classes, new activities—where members and nonmembers can build friendships?*

A: Good question. Here are some ideas for starting new side doors at your church:

- *Find the passion.* Everyone in your church cares deeply about something—sometimes several things. Such passion generally falls into one of two categories: recreational or developmental. The first relates to how people like to spend their free time. The second relates to major life issues.
- *Hold an "exploratory" meeting.* Invite three or more people who share the same passion to a brainstorming session to discuss the idea of your church starting a new ministry for people who [area of passion]. Explain that one of the purposes is to build friendships with nonmembers through connecting around a common interest. If there is any enthusiasm, take the next step.
- *Research other churches.* Chances are good that there are churches that have already developed a creative ministry in the area you are considering. Search out any other churches that might have a ministry for people with that particular interest. Then compare notes with others who have done similar research.
- *Brainstorm.* At your next meeting, discuss what such a ministry might look like in your church five years from today. If there are at least three people willing to help birth a new ministry (side door) in your church, develop a timeline with dates and events for the next year.
- *Agree that in one year the new ministry will be evaluated.* Take time to look at how well the new ministry

is fulfilling its stated purpose. If it's meeting expectations, keep it going. If not, have the courage to drop it and try again. Think of it as an experiment. Some experiments fail, but that's all right. Start a new side door ministry. One of them will begin reaching new people.

There is, of course, much more involved in creating a fully functioning side door ministry. But a majority of effective, growing churches today have a wonderful variety of side doors that grew out of the passion of one or more members and became well-traveled entry paths to life in Christ and a local church.

7

ADMINISTRATING A CHURCH

Fund Your Ministry

Q: *Money is the one topic I don't like to preach or talk about. How should I begin training my congregation to be generous givers?*

A: You are no different from other pastors. It's uncomfortable to talk about money, but it's crucial that you do so. Money is a common topic in the Bible, and in his Sermon on the Mount in Matthew 6, Jesus teaches that money is a key aspect of discipleship (vv. 19–24), that discipline in stewardship stretches one's faith (vv. 25–30), and that growing as a steward extends one's legacy (vv. 31–34).

Principles of Giving

Q: *What are the basics of stewardship?*

A: Giving is an act of generosity. It is not a function of wealth (2 Cor. 8:1–7); rather, it is a mark of a true follower of Christ (2 Cor. 8:8–15). The fundamental insight is *people give to vision more than to pay bills.* Vision is a picture of a viable future for the church. As leaders model and invest their lives in the vision, it serves as an invitation for others to give financially too (1 Chron. 29:1–20). We see an example of this when Moses collected materials for building the tabernacle in Exodus 35:4–36:7. God's leaders imparted a vision and exemplified giving, which led to a fully funded ministry.

Here are five ideas that might be helpful to you.

1. Financially healthy churches balance allocations.
- Education: 10 to 15 percent
- International missions: 10–15 percent
- Fixed costs: 10–15 percent
- Mortgage or debt reduction: 15–25 percent
- Salaries and benefits: 35–45 percent

2. People are motivated to give from six pockets.
- *General bills* pocket
- *Missions* pocket
- *Program* pocket
- *Benevolence* pocket
- *Facility* pocket
- *Projects* pocket

3. People give when they are trained to give in a systematic way.
- Leaders give first and set the example.
- Give to others and cultivate generosity.

- Talk to your donors in a nonthreatening tone and with an attitude of service. Say "thank you" and say it often.
- Use technology such as pay stations and online giving options.
- Invite guest speakers to speak about giving.

4. **People give from cash and assets.** A good example of this is seen in Acts 4:36–37, where Barnabas "sold a field" and brought the money to the apostles. The average North American has 9 percent cash and 91 percent assets.

5. **People give when they have different ways to give.**
   - Check or cash offering
   - Online platforms (e.g., PayPal)
   - Pay stations
   - Automatic deductions (e.g., weekly, monthly)
   - Direct contributions (e.g., Venmo)

Build Donor Trust

Q: People are not tithing or giving to our church in a consistent manner. How can I build trust so financial stewardship becomes consistent?

A: Donors give to organizations they trust; they won't give to organizations they don't trust. Donors give a lot to organizations they trust a lot; they give little to organizations they trust a little. What convinces a donor to trust you?

- Donors extend trust to organizations that have their outcomes assessed by outside companies.
- Donors extend trust to organizations that do good things and tell others about it.
- Donors extend trust to organizations that spend most of their money on accomplishing their mission rather than on administration (administrivia).
- Donors extend trust to organizations they hear about and that have name recognition.[1]

Budget for Growth

Q: A fellow pastor told me his church has never had a budget. The church lives week to week, which doesn't sound healthy to me. My church has always used a budget, but the process has become stilted, allowing for no fresh vision to be funded. What can I do to break out of the doldrums?

A: A budget is established based on the ministry goals of the church. Before setting a budget, it is essential to ask, "What does God want us to do as a church this year?"

After establishing your goals, follow these steps to set your budget.

1. Project your church's income for the coming year.
   - Calculate average income per person for the previous year.
   - Calculate current growth rate.

---

1. Michael Jaffarian, "How to Get Your Donors to Trust You—and Give More," Jaffarian's Little Newsletter on NonProfits and Research, July 13, 2021, https://michaeljaffarian.substack.com/p/how-to-get-your-donors-to-trust-you.

- Establish a faith goal by multiplying average income times expected growth.
2. Develop a faith financial plan.
   - Start from scratch. Don't look at last year's budget.
   - Determine salary package increases and total for all staff.
   - Determine fixed expenses.
   - Subtract salary and fixed expense totals from the established financial faith goal. The remainder is the amount you have for program and ministry expenses.
   - Ask each ministry leader to prepare a list of projected expenses for their area in order of priority.
   - Total the requested funds and compare for projected income.
   - Make necessary adjustments based on priorities and review with leaders.
3. Get approval for the budget.
   - Review the proposed budget with the church board and obtain approval.
   - Present the proposed budget to the church as needed.

Control Expenses

Q: I barely manage my own financial affairs. What is a basic process for managing a church's financial contributions?

A: It is important to monitor and track your church's financial plan. I suggest you track worship attendance, weekly offerings, and disbursements to establish patterns.

Once you have enough data to observe patterns in each of these three areas, analyze your cash flow. Be aware of where the "critical level" is in case you need to make cutbacks in ministry to remain solvent. The critical level is the amount of monthly income your church must have to stay in operation. The total includes staff salaries, rent or mortgage payments, taxes, and utilities.

If you are having problems with cash flow, only spend what was brought in last month. Hold one month in reserve. Make a priority list of which ministry expenses will be paid first and which ones will be trimmed in an emergency.

Account for and protect those involved with the church's money by separating accounting functions between counters, depositors, and treasurers, keeping financial functions in different family units, and monitoring all financial transactions. Be certain two or more people count and verify all receipts, and audit all accounts yearly.

8

LEADING A BOARD

Develop the Board

Q: The last church I attended always had conflict with the board. Are boards really needed in a church?

A: Team ministry is modeled in Scripture; boards are not. However, modern church boards came into being for several reasons:

- The early apostles appear to model a type of group decision-making similar to modern board structures (see Acts 6:1–7).
- The fact that the Holy Spirit fills every believer leads some churches to teach that more people should be involved in decision-making, and boards allow for greater participation.
- Boards often provide for shared responsibility and accountability.
- The need to do church decently and in order causes some to use a board structure of some type.

- Modern nonprofit corporations require a board of directors.

Q: So, if boards are required as part of a nonprofit corporation, what are their essential responsibilities?

A: Boards have both general responsibilities and legal responsibilities. The general responsibilities of a church board include:

- Oversee calling and evaluating the lead (senior) pastor. Note that a board should have just one employee: the lead pastor.
- Review the budget and financial plan regularly to make certain they are consistent with the church's mission, values, and policies.
- Design processes to monitor the legal, ethical, and financial solvency of the church.
- Set broad policies and make certain the ministry is carried out to fulfill them.
- Regularly report the church's activities and financial condition to all donors.
- Clearly describe the lines of authority (i.e., who reports to whom).
- Keep written records of all proceedings, decisions, and meetings.

Legal Responsibilities

Q: To my recollection, the board has never talked about its legal responsibilities. I'd like to do some board training. What are the essential legal requirements for a board?

A: Legal responsibilities are divided between fiduciary and transactional duties.

Fiduciary Responsibility: "Duty of Care"

- Board members have a duty to care for the church corporation in a reasonable and prudent manner.
- Board members must always act for the good and in the best interests of the church corporation.
- Fiduciary responsibility normally includes the total oversight of staff, activities, and assets of the corporation.
- Board members may employ outside agents (e.g., consultants, lawyers, CPAs), but in no way may they abdicate responsibility by failing to attend meetings, read reports, or monitor the activities of the corporation.

Transactional Responsibility: "Duty of Loyalty"

- Board members have a duty of loyalty, which means a board member must avoid "self-dealing."
- A related concept is "conflict of interest." Whenever a board member could personally benefit from a transaction that the church engages in, it is a conflict of interest.
- If a board member's personal involvement or interest in a church transaction takes precedence over the best interests of the church, then self-dealing has occurred.
- In general, board members may not engage in any transaction that brings private benefit or inurement

to themselves, their family members, or any organization in which they are involved.

A board must therefore establish written guidelines that clearly outline fiduciary and transactional responsibilities of the board members. A board must also develop written policies on how it will function and then train all board members in these policies on an annual basis.

Ideal Board Member

Q: The church I serve chooses board members who are not qualified. However, we have trouble agreeing on what are the best qualifications for serving on the board. What do you recommend?

A: There are no perfect board members, but it's wise to look at a prospective candidate's character, beliefs, skills, and experience.

Character

- Meets the biblical qualifications of 1 Timothy 3 and Titus 1.
- Is God-oriented rather than self-oriented.
- Is a person of prayer.
- Is committed to honesty, openness, and excellence.
- Is a discerning critical thinker without being judgmental.
- Shows faith large enough for the board's vision of the future.
- Has a servant-leader attitude and is willing to work hard.

Beliefs

- Agrees with the church's mission, vision, values, and statement of faith, and holds a Christian worldview.
- Is supportive of the pastoral leadership and enthusiastic about the church's future.

Skills

- Gives financially to the church (10 percent minimum).
- Accepts the time commitment involved in board leadership.
- Brings one or more of three resources to the board: wealth, wisdom, or willingness to work.
- Is actively involved in at least one major church ministry.

Experience

- Has a record of successful leadership in other fields of work or service.
- Can work as part of a team.
- Has a wide network of friends or professional contacts.
- Can delegate effectively.
- If married, has a spouse who is supportive of him or her serving on the church board. In addition, the spouse is also a biblically qualified person who can maintain confidentiality and has a positive perspective about the church.
- Has no hidden agendas or conflicts of interest.

Board Expectations

Q: *Most people on our board work full-time at their job while also volunteering at church. What expectations are reasonable for me to have of them?*

A: The average volunteer gives two to three hours a week in service to their church. Board members often donate up to eight hours a week, some even more. Here are some expectations from two viewpoints.

What the Lead Pastor Expects from Board Members

- Do not surprise the pastor.
- Do not interfere with the staff. Observe but don't get in the way of the staff. Remember, "Eyes in, fingers out."
- Support the pastor privately and publicly.
- Give and raise money.
- Care about the pastor's professional growth.
- Care about the pastor's personal and family well-being.
- Be honest and direct; keep in touch with the pastor.
- Retain the long view; keep a positive perspective on the church.
- Focus attention on important issues; ignore petty issues.
- Understand the mission of the church.

What Board Members Expect from the Lead Pastor

- Do not surprise the board; provide timely information.
- Be honest, open, and direct.

- Be proactive and take the lead in strategic planning for vision, values, and goals.
- Implement board policies efficiently and effectively.
- Articulate vision for the church.
- Listen well.
- Help the board understand how the church works.
- Tell the board what you need.
- Demonstrate the ability to take constructive criticism.
- Raise money.
- Respect the board's policy-making role.
- Lead in recruiting and training board members.

Q: *How can I hold the board members accountable?*

A: Once a year ask the board members to complete a statement affirming their commitment to your church. I've included a sample statement below.

BOARD MEMBER AFFIRMATION STATEMENT

Along with all other board members, I submit this affirmation statement, understanding that the spirit of this is to remind us all of our commitment to service and support of (name of church).

☐ I continue to be fully supportive of the mission and purpose of (name of church), as well as the (name of board) and pastoral leadership.

☐ I affirm by my signature below acceptance of our Statement of Faith (attached).

☐ I understand and agree to submit a Conflict of Interest Questionnaire (attached). In so doing I am providing full disclosure of any conflict of interest between (name of church) and me.

☐ I understand that board participation requires the equivalent of 10–12 days per year of my time, including homework, special assignments, and meetings. I am able to give that amount of time during the next year and will be present at no fewer than ten of the twelve meetings.

☐ I understand that attendance at the annual board retreat is expected and that I must attend a minimum of two retreats out of three.

☐ I recognize the need for full board participation in contributing financially to (name of church). I also recognize that I am strongly encouraged to contribute at least 10 percent of my yearly income to (name of church). Therefore, I will contribute financially to the work of (name of church) during each year I am on the board, and I will also encourage others to do the same.

☐ I will speak with the board officers about a volunteer resignation if anything should occur during my board tenure that would not allow me to honor my intentions of being a positive contributor to the board.

Signature_____ Date_____

Q: We've experienced some discord on our board due to conflicts of interest. How might I limit such conflicts?

A: At the first board meeting of the year, ask board members to complete a conflict of interest survey. This will alert you to any possible conflicts of interest while alerting the member to times when they should recuse themselves from participating in discussions and decisions. I've included a sample survey below.

BOARD MEMBER CONFLICT OF INTEREST SURVEY

Are you an officer, director, or board member of any company or organization that (name of church) has business dealings with?

Yes _____ No _____

If you answered yes, please list the names of such organizations or companies and the manner in which each is involved with (name of church).

_____

_____

_____

Do you or any member of your family have a financial interest in or receive remuneration from (name of church) or any business organization with which (name of church) has business dealings?

Yes _____ No _____

If you answered yes, please supply the following information:

a. Name(s) of the business organization(s) in which such interest is held and the person(s) by whom such interest is held.

b. Nature and amount of each such financial interest, remuneration, or income.

_____

_____

_____

Did you or any member of your family receive, during the past twelve months, any gifts, loans, or money from any source from which (name of church) buys goods or services, or with which (name of church) has significant business dealings?

Yes _____ No _____

If you answered yes, list any such gifts, loans, or moneys:

Source name   Approximate value

_____   _____

_____   _____

_____   _____

Is any member of your immediate or extended family employed by (name of church)?

Yes _____ No _____

If you answered yes, note the person's name, their role or job, and their relationship to you.

Name   Role or job   Relationship to you

_____   _____   _____

_____   _____   _____

_____   _____   _____

I certify that the foregoing information is true and complete to the best of my knowledge.

Signature_____Date _____

How to Master Meetings

Q: *The thought of attending another meeting creates knots in my stomach. Would you share some ways of effectively leading meetings?*

A: Meetings are one of the best communication systems available to leaders. Meetings can also be one of the most frustrating communication systems known to leaders. Here are some reasons that meetings have such a bad reputation:

- They are badly run.
- They often go too long.
- They are often used as excuses to avoid making decisions.
- They often waste time when important things need to be done.

Consider the following checkpoints to improve meetings:

- Meetings have an agenda. Remember, if there's no agenda, there's no meeting!
- Meetings are built around a simple agenda, such as:
  - Items for declaration
  - Items for decision
  - Items for discussion
- Problem-solving meetings are built around a process agenda, such as:
  - State the decision to be made
  - Clarify the issue
  - Develop criteria
  - List options

- Evaluate options against criteria
- Make a decision
- Meetings are attended by the *right* people.
- Meeting participants come well prepared.
- The objective of the meeting is well-defined and of a nature that will benefit from a group discussion and/or decision.
- The meeting is not a substitute for direct confrontation with unpleasant people.
- Leaders understand and work with the standard meeting life cycle.
  - **Warm-up**: Initial fifteen minutes for members to arrive, relax, and get ready for the meeting.
  - **Rev-up**: The heart of the meeting time, lasting thirty to ninety minutes. This is when most discussion occurs and decisions are made. It's wise to limit decisions to just three items per meeting.
  - **Wrap-up**: The last fifteen to thirty minutes when energy dissipates. Decisions made during this time are of poor quality.

Q: How might I make meetings productive rather than a waste of time?

A: Church leaders and volunteers spend a great deal of time in meetings. Unfortunately, meetings can be frustrating since they often begin late, go too long, and produce more discussion than action. Here are steps you can take to create better meetings.

1. *Begin by scheduling meetings at odd times.* For example, starting at 10:50 a.m. is better than starting at

11:00 a.m. Doing this helps focus the starting time in people's minds.

2. *Start on time and end on time.* When you make a habit of starting and ending on time, people show up. No matter who is missing, start the meeting on time. Close the door when it is time to begin as a signal that the starting time is important. When it is time to end, bring the meeting to a close. Continue any discussion at the next meeting.

3. *Plan your agenda around three items: declaration, decision, and discussion.* In the first part of the meeting, declare items of information that need no discussion or decisions. Next, move to items that need decisions. Most people can only make three major decisions in one meeting, so if you need to make more than three decisions, schedule a second meeting. Finally, move to discussion as the meeting nears the end. People will naturally want to finish on time, and this will help curtail overly long discussions. If further discussion is needed, continue it at the next meeting.

4. *Focus on the most important decisions first.* Let people know that items of interest to them will be dealt with early in the meeting. By doing this, you will motivate those who are chronically late to show up on time.

5. *Speak privately to those who are chronically late.* When people are habitually late, talk with them outside of the meeting. Explain that their input is important and that you value their insights.

6. *Follow through on decisions by assigning them to specific individuals for completion.* Teams and

committees are good at discussing issues and making decisions but poor at follow-through. Delegate all action items to specific people and ask them to report what they have done during the information or discussion time at the next meeting.

7. *Take time to build community.* Meetings tend to drain people of their spiritual vitality. Do take time to share personal stories and pray for one another, but be sure to get the work done or people will become even more frustrated.

9

MAKING DISCIPLES

Definition of a Disciple

Q: Discipleship is a buzzword today. My colleagues talk about it every time we get together. Yet, no one seems to do more than talk. What are some of the core aspects of effective disciple-making?

A: In the diving competition at the 2016 Summer Olympics in Rio, one of the commentators made an interesting remark about Team China. He said that in training divers, the first thing the Chinese coaches do is teach them how to enter the water from whichever diving apparatus they are competing on (springboard or platform). Prior to any work on flips, turns, somersaults, and other aspects of technique, divers are coached on how to enter the water. The result is that Chinese divers enter the water with minimal splash, and minimal splash is a critical element of scoring high marks.

In essence, the Chinese divers start with the end in mind. Everything else is built on the conclusion of the dive. If they know how to end well, everything leading up to that provides a solid performance.

This same principle applies to the disciple-making process. You need to know what you are looking for in a disciple. What does a disciple look like? What actions, attitudes, and attributes do you want in a follower of Jesus? You need to define what you want to accomplish and how you are going to do it. Clarity as to the result will inform the process you put in place to get there.

A disciple is an individual who is following Christ, being changed by Christ, and committed to the mission of Christ. It is the drive to produce these attributes that informs the disciple-making process.

The most basic characteristic of a disciple is obedience. This is seen in John 2:1–12, the story of Jesus turning water into wine. Mary, the mother of Jesus, tells the servants, "Do whatever he tells you" (Matt. 2:5 NLT). Obeying Jesus's instructions without hesitation is the primary mark of a disciple. For all the effort that goes into defining a disciple, obedience is an observable action.

Q: *Must the pastor lead a disciple-making effort?*

A: Disciple-making begins with following, and a pastor must set the example in this. You cannot make disciples of Jesus unless you are his disciple. You cannot challenge others to follow Christ unless you follow him. The best way to create a disciple-making movement is to model how to be a good follower.

Following is the most underrated form of leadership. Paul told those he led, "Follow my example, as I follow Christ" (1 Cor. 11:1 NLT).

As the pastor, you are to lead your church in following Jesus. You are the genesis, epicenter, and core of the disciple-making aspect of your church. You must be in a discipling relationship and you must be discipling others. It will be from your modeling and living as a disciple that your church will progress toward fitness in this area. It is out of your connection with God that you are able to influence others to connect with God. What are you doing to increase being influenced by God?

Principles of Disciple-Making[1]

Q: Okay, what are the essential principles for making disciples?

A: There are five key principles that influence and determine the process, structure, and material for effective disciple-making:

1. *Effective disciple-making is relational.* It must have an element of life on life. People are discipled in relationship, not in the transference of knowledge or content.
2. *Effective disciple-making is biblical.* The Word of God is the central basis for making disciples. A disciple is a follower of Christ. How better to understand who you follow than to read about who Jesus is, how he thinks, and what he did during his time on earth.
3. *Effective disciple-making is applicable.* If a disciple-making process does not impact how people live in

---

1. The content under this heading is adapted from Phil Stevenson, "5 Principles for Effective Disciple-Making in the 21st Century," Seedbed, August 15, 2016, https://seedbed.com/5-principles-for-effective-disciple-making-in-the-21st-century/. Used with permission.

the world, then it is merely religious ritual. Disciples bring the kingdom of God into the realms of life where they have been placed.

4. *Effective disciple-making is accountable.* Accountability is the least considered aspect in many a disciple-making process. Accountability goes beyond getting assignments completed, while holding those serious in following Christ to living out that followership in daily life.

5. *Effective disciple-making is reproducible.* Reproducing other disciples is often the missing piece of disciple-making. Genuine disciple-making has happened when other disciples have been multiplied. The going and making of disciples is a lifelong process.

These five principles are the filter used in developing, implementing, and evaluating disciple-making in our ministries. Consistently ask the five disciple-making questions:

- What is the relational impact?
- How is the Bible used?
- How are you applying what is being discovered in daily life?
- How are people being held accountable?
- How is what you are doing being reproduced?

Disciple-making is the call of every Christ follower. The call to "go and make disciples" (Matt. 28:19 NLT) continues to be the intent of Jesus's mandate to his church.

Mentoring[2]

Q: I've never had a mentor. Why do I need one?

A: Having a coach is a predictor of success. This should not surprise us. Most professional trades have apprenticeships. Medical professions require internships. Even the Bible reveals that ministry success or fruitfulness often comes out of mentoring relationships. Good examples of this include Moses and Joshua, Elijah and Elisha, Paul and Timothy, Naomi and Ruth, and of course Jesus and his disciples.

Q: What is mentoring?

A: Former American politician John C. Crosby once said that a mentor is "a brain to pick, an ear to listen, and a push in the right direction." At the foundational level, mentoring is a face-to-face meeting of two people in which one shares their knowledge, wisdom, and advice with another. Mentoring is more than simply talking together or having a Bible study or playing games over coffee. While these types of activities are excellent, they are not mentoring. True mentoring involves a strategic goal of helping a person improve a skill. When mentoring relationships are analyzed, we typically find a younger or less experienced person initiates contact with an older or more experienced person with a specific request for help in developing a specific skill.

---

2. The content under this heading is adapted from Gary L. McIntosh. "Mentoring Relationships," *The Good Book Blog*, June 6, 2018, https://www.biola.edu/blogs/good-book-blog/2018/mentoring-relationships.

Q: How do I start in mentoring others?

A: While there are many ways to engage in a mentoring relationship, here are some basic guidelines you should keep in mind.

- *Set the tone.* It's up to the mentor to set the tone. Do you want the relationship to be relaxed and informal or businesslike and formal? Will you let the mentee become like one of your family members, or will you keep a boundary between home and work? Will you simply invite the mentee along to observe you in ministry situations, or will you spend time sharing your personal story?
- *Define the expectations early in the relationship.* Who will pay for the coffee? How often will you meet? How long will your meetings be? What will be the level of accountability? What is the purpose of the relationship? Is there a fee for your time, or are you giving your time to them for free?
- *Ask good questions.* A mentor is not just an "answer person" but a "question person." Perhaps the most important quality of a good mentor is their ability to ask good questions. Consider some of the following questions as examples:

  What are you thinking about?

  What is stirring inside of you?

  What is working in your life and ministry?

  What is not working in your life and ministry?

  How is your sense of God's call being clarified?

  What are some new things you could try?

Making Disciples

As you assess your growth, where do you see areas you need to work on?

How may I help you?

How has that experience shaped you?

How has (or might) God use your past pain to prepare you for the future?

- *Nudge in the right direction.* Many people approach a new task with fear. Thus, a good mentor serves as a confidence builder, often by pushing mentees in new directions. Push mentees through their discomfort to take responsibility for their actions. Ask questions such as:

What are you going to do about it?

When are you going to get started?

What are your next steps?

Recruiting

Q: Volunteer recruitment is a problem in my church. We ask for assistance every week but get little response. How can we more effectively recruit ministry volunteers?

A: One key aspect of leading a church is recruiting people to serve Christ. It's important not to confuse recruiting with calling. Every Christian is called to minister. The only questions are how, where, when, or to whom, but not whether. Recruitment is getting people who are already called to go to work. Consider the following guidelines as you recruit ministry volunteers:

- *Start with letting people know of your vision, goals, and plans.* Then watch for those who are following or show interest in what you are doing.

- *Discover those who naturally lead.* Notice who others like to quote or joke about or tell stories about. Natural leaders have a natural following.
- *Look for evidence of a person's calling or interest.* What are they saying they want to become? What courses are they signing up for in school? What books, blogs, or articles do they read?
- *Keep in mind the qualifications and personality strengths of the individuals you desire to recruit.* For example:
  - What level of work is required? Are you recruiting for an unskilled position or an executive type of position?
  - What personality traits are needed? Are you looking for someone who can work alone or someone to work on a team?
  - What amount of experience is necessary? Are you looking for someone with lots of experience or someone who is new to the job?
  - What length of commitment is important? Are you looking for someone to commit long-term or short-term? Is the person afraid of commitment or are they ready to commit?
  - What mix of giftedness is helpful? Are you looking for gifts of teaching, administration, serving, caring, giving, leading, or something else?
- *Look for people who are already motivated.* Don't spend time trying to motivate those who are unwilling to become volunteers. Simply work with as many willing people as you have. Don't be overwhelmed by

Making Disciples

a person's education, background, appearance, or giftedness. Some people look better than they perform. Identify quantifiable ways to assess what they are producing in ministry.

- *Watch what people do; don't just listen to what they say.* Time is on your side. See if they demonstrate commitment. Are they on time every week? Do they follow through on what they say? Remember, it is easier to identify and recruit people to ministry than it is to remove them from ministry.
- *Communicate the true picture of the job to be accomplished.* Write out a specific ministry description. Tell potential recruits about the training requirements. Let them know the cost in time and energy. Sharing the real challenges of the work will draw them to commitment.
- *Provide training for the work.* Training comes in three different ways: formal, informal, and modeling. Formal training involves educational classes or seminars. This is best done after a person has already been involved in ministry for a while. Informal training takes place as a person does ministry and then participates in group discussions or one-on-one conversations. Modeling takes place as people observe others doing ministry and then reproduce what they see.

  In most church situations it is best to train by modeling. Start by assigning a recruit to someone already involved in ministry. Encourage them to shadow another person and observe what ministry is all about. Let them ask questions and make suggestions based on what they see. In time let them do more and more of the work until they become confident to do it alone. The overall goal is to have them succeed, enjoy the work, and want to continue. People usually have a greater thirst for training as they are involved in direct ministry.

- *Deploy people in ministry.* When deploying new people in ministry, use four steps. First, let them watch others doing the particular ministry. Second, let them do the ministry together with someone more experienced. Third, let them do the ministry alone while the more experienced person watches. Fourth, let them do the ministry with no one watching them.

- *Monitor each person's progress.* Continue to give feedback as the person moves forward in ministry. Ask specific questions rather than just "How are things going?" The questions you ask set the standard to which they'll seek to perform. Surprise them by showing up and watching them for twenty minutes, then compliment them on some aspect of their work the next day.

- *Nurture new recruits so they'll feel appreciated.* Continually talk about your vision and explain how their ministry contributes to its accomplishment. Ask their counsel for any changes in their area of ministry, and bring them into collegial meetings with others in similar roles.

Recruitment is an ongoing process. Put some of these ideas into practice this week.

Delegation

Q: Managing my time is a challenge. I know I should be delegating work to others, but how do I do this?

A: Sooner or later all leaders discover limitations in their capacity to handle growing responsibilities. Most leaders find they have limits in one or more of the following areas:

- The *amount of work* they can do
- The *number of people* they can work with
- The *number of details* they can remember
- The *number of activities* they can participate in

As ministry grows, the ever-expanding responsibilities of the leader will always outpace their personal capacity to carry them out. If a leader seeks to expand capacity, it may lead to illness as they attempt to do more than is possible. A leader could lessen responsibilities, but a person of vision won't do so. Thus, the only reasonable option is to delegate certain responsibilities to others.

Q: What is delegation?

A: Delegation is entrusting another person to perform specific work with commensurate authority and with a mutual understanding of the expected results. This definition demonstrates four elements of effective delegation:

1. Passing along a task to another person
2. Identifying clear and specific duties to be performed
3. Giving commensurate power or authority to do the task
4. Asking for proper reporting of the finished task

Q: Is delegation biblical?

A: Delegation is seen in numerous places throughout the Bible. It's practiced among the triune Godhead (John 5:22, 27; 14:26; 17:4–12) and in the angelic realms (Heb. 1:14). God delegated care of the garden of Eden to Adam (Gen. 1:28). Delegation is seen in the leadership of Israel (Exod. 18:17–23; 1 Kings 4:1–19), in the life of Christ (Matt. 10; John 19:26–27), and in the commission to witness (Matt. 28:18–20; Acts 1:8; 2 Cor. 5:20). Further, the use of delegation is observed in the life of the church (Acts 6:1–7; 20:28; Rom. 12:3–8; 1 Cor. 12–14; Heb. 13:17), in human government (Rom. 13), and in families (Eph. 5:6; 1 Pet. 3).

Q: When should delegation be used?

A: You should delegate in three specific situations:

1. *When there are routine procedures that another person can handle.* This includes tasks such as filing, correspondence, phone calls, emails, record-keeping, errands, purchases, making photocopies, and a host of similar activities.

2. *When a particular task or responsibility is appropriate for a committee or officer.* For example, handling requests from missionaries to speak, ordering new checks, or setting up tables in a classroom. These and similar tasks are best delegated to a team, officer, or volunteer.

3. *When a task could be done well by another person.* For example, ask a sports enthusiast to lead the sports program, ask those who have a heart for children to lead the children's ministry, and ask the person who reads a great deal to gather sermon illustrations for you.

Making Disciples

Q: I have trouble letting go of even the smallest tasks. How do I begin to delegate?

A: Start small by delegating one item each week over the next month. In doing so, you'll have four fewer things on your to-do list at the end of the month.

- *Select a task you'd like to give away* and determine the exact dimensions of the assignment (e.g., what it entails, how much time it takes, the degree of authority needed).
- *Choose the most capable person available.* If you have time, select a person who can be trained in the task, as delegation is a fine way to develop leaders.
- *Make the assignment.* If made verbally, be sure to follow up with a written note or email. Explain *why* the person was selected, *what* the task is, and the *results* expected.
- *Provide needed support.* For example, supply any necessary funds, let others know this person is overseeing the task, and brief anyone who needs to know.
- *Check on progress.* When the task is simple, ask "How are things going?" When the job is complex, ask for regular written reports and meetings.
- *Evaluate achievement.* Review progress from time to time and offer praise or suggestions.

Q: What problems might I encounter when delegating?

A: There are four problems that arise when delegating work to others.

1. Taking back the delegated task. This is perhaps the major challenge one faces when beginning to delegate. For example, the person to whom the task is given isn't completing it correctly or fast enough, so you start doing it again.
2. Tasks are under-delegated—that is, you don't give enough away. For example, the task is assigned without enough authority for the person to do the job.
3. Tasks are over-delegated—that is, you give away too much and end up losing contact, oversight, and influence.
4. The process of delegating is confusing. Clarity is missing regarding the actual task, timing, authority, and available support.

Q: *Are there tasks I should not delegate to others?*

A: Yes. In the process of deciding to delegate, you should retain

- the power to discipline
- responsibility for maintaining morale
- tasks that require your skill and training
- tasks that involve information that is confidential
- tasks that are large and serious

10

DESIGNING WORSHIP

Dynamics of Worship

Q: *Congregational worship is central to a healthy church. What constitutes a good worship service?*

A: Defining an effective worship service is difficult. However, we all seem to know when we are in one. From a practical point of view, an effective worship service is celebrative—that is, a celebration of God's attributes and his work in the world and in our lives. What, then, makes a worship service celebrative?

- *People attend.* Celebrative services attract people who come because they desire to attend rather than because they must attend.
- *People bring others.* Celebrative services encourage attendees to invite their friends and family to come with them.

- *People participate.* Celebrative services create an environment where singing, giving, praying, and other aspects of worship are entered into with enthusiasm.
- *People listen.* Celebrative services hold the attention of worshipers throughout the entire time of worship.
- *People grow.* Celebrative services challenge individuals to make biblical decisions that affect their daily living.[1]

Q: What does it take to make an effective worship service?

A: Most pastors are educated to believe effective worship just happens. For many pastors, the only item they focus on is the sermon. However, when the overall quality of the worship service is elevated, attendance increases. It's possible to take steps to make a worship service celebrative. Think about using some of the following ideas:

- *Build around one theme.* Celebrative worship services have a sense of unity that is best achieved by building the entire service around one basic theme. To enhance worship services, identify the broad theme you wish to communicate to your congregation. Be sure to connect your music, message, introductions, transitional comments, and even announcements to the theme. Look for logical content and emotional flow. Let the content of the Scripture, prayers, readings, and transitions contribute to the theme.
- *Plan for participation.* Celebrative worship services involve the congregation in meaningful ways. To

1. Glen Martin & Gary McIntosh, "Worship," Apostolic Information Service, November 12, 2008, https://www.apostolic.edu/worship-2/.

Designing Worship

enhance worship services, build in ways for people to be involved. Allow for singing, clapping, standing, listening, shouting, greeting, gesturing, lifting hands, kneeling, completing a study guide, praying, talking, laughing, crying, responding, thanking, pondering, promising, confessing, lamenting, and other ways of participating.

- *Develop a sense of flow.* Celebrative worship services have a clear flow and sense of direction. To enhance worship services, think through how each part of the service relates to the whole. Each part of the service should connect logically to the next part to have a sense of direction.

- *Speed up the pace.* Celebrative worship services move along fast enough to keep people's attention on the theme. To enhance worship services, use both upbeat tempos and reflective tempos to focus people's attention.

- *Eliminate dead time.* Celebrative worship services move smoothly between various parts of the service with very little dead time where people may lose attention. To enhance worship services, design good transitions between each element.

- *Use variety.* Celebrative worship services use a variety of worship elements to maintain everyone's interest, enjoyment, and connection to the theme. To enhance worship services, include a variety of elements such as drama, Scripture reading, congregational response, videos, and interviews.

- *Plan your worship service.* Celebrative worship services are designed weeks in advance. To enhance worship services, recruit and involve a worship team in organizing services six to eight weeks ahead of time.

- *Engage a worship team for creativity.* Celebrative worship services use the creative talents of multiple people. To enhance worship services, meet weekly with a worship team to brainstorm ideas and plan for future services.
- *Appeal to the mind and the heart.* Celebrative worship services balance content and emotion. A focus on biblical content without engaging the congregation's emotions makes for *hollow* worship. A focus on the congregation's emotions without engaging biblical content makes for *shallow* worship. Both mind and heart engagement are needed. To enhance worship services, make creative use of music, rhythm, movement, stories, illustrations, and other experiential tools. We keep worship authentic by involving people's hearts as well as their heads.
- *Design a worship set that is progressive.* Psalm 95 is a good model.
  - Invitation: "Come, let us sing for joy . . . let us shout aloud" (v. 1).
  - Engagement: "Let us come before him with thanksgiving" (v. 2).
  - Exaltation: "For the LORD is the great God . . . the mountain peaks belong to him" (vv. 3–4).
  - Adoration: "Come, let us bow down . . . let us kneel" (v. 6).
  - Intimacy: "For . . . we are the people of his pasture, the flock under his care" (v. 7).

Sermon

Q: Isn't the sermon the centerpiece of the worship service?

A: A good principle to remember is this: *The sermon is not the message; the message is the service.* Yet, the sermon *is* a primary part of the worship service. As such, it's crucial for a pastor to deliver the best sermon possible. Here are some ideas that may be helpful as you prepare to preach.

- *Good preachers prepare.* The best preachers spend about fifteen hours each week in sermon preparation, divided over two weeks. In the first week, the pastor spends seven to eight hours exegeting the passage(s) of Scripture to understand it. The big idea or eternal principle is defined and a tentative outline is laid out. Many pastors will then let the message percolate for a week of prayerful reflection. The following week, an additional seven to eight hours are given to filling in the outline with illustrations, stories, testimonies, and other didactic techniques, as well as practicing the delivery.[2]

- *Good preachers preach 20–30 minutes.* The saying goes, "Good preachers preach 20–23 minutes; bad preachers shouldn't preach any longer." Now, some preachers do preach an hour or longer and it only seems like twenty minutes. Others, of course, preach for twenty minutes and it seems like an hour. What makes the difference is preparation and practice.

2. Gary L. McIntosh and Charles Arn, *What Every Pastor Should Know* (Baker Books, 2013), 56.

- *Good preachers are interesting.* If you're going to bore people, bore them with Shakespeare, not the Bible. Fruitful preachers live with a fear of making the Bible and God, which are relevant, seem irrelevant. Boredom is a hard thing for people to tolerate. Instead of drawing people to God, uninteresting sermons drive them from him. God is not boring, so why should our sermons be?
- *Good preachers entertain people.* Critics are prone to say pastors shouldn't entertain people, but this is a misunderstanding of terms. Entertain means "to hold one's attention," which all speakers desire to do. What pastors should not do is amuse people, which means "to be without thought." Keep people's attention but make sure to keep them thinking.
- *Good preachers listen to their people.* Some church members will tell you one thing while criticizing another. They most likely don't have preaching experience or the training to diagnose or prescribe how to help you preach better, but their comments may point out a symptom that you need to hear and address. Listen to what they are saying.
- *Good preachers offer solutions.* They spend more time giving answers than pointing out problems. It's always easier to show others what's wrong than to offer solutions, which is why many pastors spend twice as much time describing the problem as they do offering the solution. Make sure your most powerful illustrations and descriptions show people what to do.
- *Good preachers condition themselves.* There's a difference between preparing a sermon and preparing

156

yourself. A good long-distance runner does not attempt a marathon without conditioning their body ahead of time. Likewise, a pastor should not step into the pulpit or on the stage without prior conditioning. Personal submission to the Lord throughout the week is a must. Prayer, journaling, fasting, solitude, reflection, and meditation help condition one for delivering God's Word to the people.

- *Good preachers keep preaching.* Many times you won't see anything happening week to week, but the Spirit of God is working unseen beneath the surface to enliven those who hear your preaching. Being exposed to good preaching is like eating three meals a day. Most of us who eat three meals a day cannot remember what we ate last week or even yesterday. Sure, we remember an occasional fantastic meal, but most meals are not memorable. And yet, we'd be poorer if we didn't eat three meals a day. Good preaching is like that too. We don't typically see a dramatic change in people every Sunday, but over time the faithful preaching of God's Word is effective in moving people in the right direction.

Preach for a Verdict

Q: My preaching appears to be liked by the congregation—at least, I receive few complaints. Yet people just go about their lives with little change. How can I preach in a more challenging way?

A: The Gospel of Mark shows that our role as servants of Christ is to preach the good news of salvation and persuade men and women, boys and girls, to place their faith in Jesus Christ alone for salvation. Another way to say it is our role is to preach for a verdict.

Among other things, this means we must be people of action, obediently doing our part in spreading the good news about Jesus Christ, and people of persuasion, boldly declaring Jesus Christ to be the only way to salvation.

The old debates concerning human obedience and God's sovereignty in Christian mission, as well as the place of dialogue and persuasion in evangelism, are major issues in Christian outreach today. In the debate over our role and responsibility in connection with God's sovereignty in salvation, some stress that since God is sovereign and therefore sufficient to accomplish evangelism without human agency, our role is simply to bear witness through our lives to his love and grace, allowing God to bring about people's salvation in his time. According to this perspective, our role is to follow the oft-quoted maxim from St. Francis of Assisi: "Preach the gospel, and if necessary, use words." The idea is we must let our light shine and God will bring people to faith as he desires. Of course God is sovereign and does not need us to accomplish his purposes on earth. However, no Christian denies either God's sovereignty or human responsibility for preaching the good news. Indisputably God is sovereign, but he calls his people to take the gospel to the world.

The New Testament symbolism of stewards and servants is rich in this regard. "We are God's fellow workers" (1 Cor. 3:9). The Greek word translated as "fellow worker" (*sunergoi*) is a concept we see throughout the New Testament. In every case, the one given the role of worker or steward is required to be obedient. For example, in the parable of the

Designing Worship

pounds and the talents (Matt. 25:14–30; Luke 19:11–27), the master gives gifts to servants who are considered responsible agents. At the end of the story, the master holds his servants responsible for their obedience or disobedience. Those servants who obeyed received a reward, while the disobedient servant was punished.

Likewise, the apostle Paul reminds the Corinthians, "I planted, Apollos watered, but God was causing the growth" (1 Cor. 3:6 NASB). Here is the simple answer to the debate. God sovereignly brings about the growth of the church through evangelism, but his servants are held responsible. Paul notes the servant's responsibility when he says, "Now he who plants and he who waters are one; but each will receive his own reward according to his own labor. For we are God's fellow workers" (vv. 8–9). Only God in his sovereignty brings people to faith in Christ, but our role as responsible agents (stewards and servants) is to take specific action to fulfill this calling by preaching for a verdict.

We live in a diverse religious culture, which causes some Christians to back away from attempting to persuade others that Jesus Christ is the only way to heaven (John 14:6). Some even suggest that the best approach is to dialogue with others to find the common truth in all faiths while allowing individuals to come to their own conclusions about truth.

Regrettably, the concept of dialogue is quite vague. At its best, dialogue suggests a friendly, respectful discussion that seeks to persuade the other person to one's view. At its worst, however, dialogue suggests a conversation between people where neither seeks to persuade the other; rather, they dialogue purely to communicate. Dialogue becomes nothing but an attitude of respectful discussion with no agenda of converting the other person to one's point of view. The first form of dialogue is certainly biblical—that is, we should seek to persuade others with a spirit of mutual understanding. But the second concept of dialogue is decidedly not biblical, for Christians must always witness for a verdict—that is, the Christian always seeks to persuade another to believe in Jesus Christ for salvation, accept baptism, and become a responsible part of the church.

Both the Old and New Testaments model belief in the one true God rather than the gods of this world. The entire Bible presents God as the Creator and Sustainer of the world (Gen. 1:1–2:25; John 1:1–3; Col. 1:16–17). He alone is worthy of worship, as God commanded, "You shall have no other gods before Me" (Exod. 20:3). In the New Testament, people are called to make a choice for or against Jesus Christ. "The one who believes in Him is not judged; the one who does not believe has been judged already, because he has not believed in the name of the only begotten Son of God" (John 3:18 NASB). Jesus's declaration "I am the way, and the truth, and the life; no one comes to the Father but through Me" (John 14:6) demands a verdict. Jesus stressed the need to choose when he asked his disciples "Who do people say the Son of Man is?" To which Peter gave his powerful confession "You are the Christ, the Son of the living God" (John 16:13–16). Peter and the disciples made their choice. A decision must always be made: Is Jesus Christ the Savior of the world or not? Preach for a verdict!

Music

Q: What purpose does music have within the worship service?

A: Preaching does not stand alone as worship. It's supported by and communicates in large part due to its context. To concentrate on preaching without a corresponding emphasis on context often leads to less than spectacular results. A great preacher without a supporting context is hampered; an average preacher with a supporting context is empowered to communicate.

A good context is built with excellent worship music. This seems obvious when it's understood that 30 to 40 percent of worship time is allotted to music. Here are some insights for how to create a context with music to support the preaching:

- *Select music the congregation can sing.* Singability is not the only thing, but it may be the most important aspect of a good worship context. When songs are vocally too low or too high, people quit singing. The practical range for the average person is between the B-flat below middle C and the D an octave above middle C.
- *Select music that is familiar to the congregation.* An entire service of unfamiliar music will not allow the congregation to participate.
- *Select music that appeals to the aesthetics of the congregation.* This includes music that has a beat, rhythm, and tempo that fits their culture.
- *Select music that provides a mode of experience that enables people to internalize their faith.* Do not use emotion for the sake of emotion but for the congregation's discipleship.
- *Embody creative use of the arts.* This involves using different types of music, drama, painting, poetry, appropriate dance, and other performing arts, not as

an extraneous gimmick but as an integral part of the worship service.

- *Choose wisely the music you use.* There are about five thousand contemporary Christian songs available today, plus around one million hymns. Yet, the average congregation uses fewer than two hundred, and a congregation may know only 10 percent of those well (about twenty songs). Thus, you have the luxury of selecting the best and most appropriate music that meets your musical, textual, and pastoral criteria. Choose wisely.

SOME "DOS" OF WORSHIP

- Do teach the biblical basis for worship.
- Do expose people to varied worship practices and forms.
- Do take a proactive role in directing worship leaders.
- Do increase meaningful congregational performance.
- Do honor worship leaders and musicians as colleagues in ministry. They are spiritual leaders, not just technicians.
- Do use music that is joyful and spiritually edifying.
- Do attend worship conferences with your entire worship team.
- Do use music that is biblically and musically sound.
- Do think of the entire collective congregation as the main human agent in worship.
- Do think of God as the main audience of the congregation's worship.
- Do start and end the worship service strong.
- Do write out transitions ahead of time.

Multiple Services

Q: I see many churches offering multiple worship services. Is this a good idea?

A: While offering a second worship service is not a new idea, growing churches find that having multiple worship services can be a good way to serve people in our fast-paced world.

Q: Why add multiple services?

A: It's important for church leaders to consider *why* they need to add an additional worship service before thinking about the *how*, *where*, and *when*. In general, multiple services . . .

- *Provide options.* The one-size-fits-all worship service is a thing of the past. Adding a new worship service is a way to provide choices in church ministry.
- *Expand space.* Multiple services allow a church to use its current facilities multiple times without incurring the costs of a building program.
- *Allow for growth.* Numerical growth is capped in an overcrowded auditorium. Adding even one additional worship service allows a church to grow by 20 to 80 percent.
- *Enlarge faith.* Churches that add additional worship services place an emphasis on reaching newer members, which takes vision and faith.
- *Increase workers.* Adding a second worship service opens new ministry opportunities where people may serve. As a rule, for every person who has a ministry role or task, another two or three people will attend the worship service with them.

- *Reach new people.* Adding additional worship services with different times, styles, and approaches attracts new people who do not normally attend.
- *Maintain morale.* The changing preferences of people regarding styles of music and dress and time of worship are too complex to address in one worship service. Having multiple services allows a church to tailor the worship experience to people's various expectations.

Q: When should a new worship service be added?

A: To be most successful, it's best to add an additional service when . . .

- *The momentum is rising.* One of the mistakes churches make is adding a new service after it's too late. The key is to add the service as growth momentum is rising rather than after it has peaked and is declining.
- *The morale is high.* If a church is experiencing a period of discouragement or conflict, it should resolve those issues before moving toward multiple services. Adding a new service is a step of faith that is best accomplished when morale is positive.
- *The moment is right.* Attempts to add additional services fail due to wrong timing. The best chance of success happens when a second service is started during the normal growth cycles of the church year—for example, in September and October or January and February.

Q: What are the major issues I should consider before adding an additional worship service?

A: Any church wishing to begin a new worship service will do well to think through the following issues:

- *Style of service.* The major issue facing churches is whether a new service will be identical to or a different style from the other service(s). The key factor is the diversity of the congregation. The more diverse the congregation, the more likely a new service will succeed if it has a different style.
- *Balancing attendance.* An issue often overlooked is whether attendance at all services will be balanced. The key factors are the seating capacity of the worship space, the makeup of the congregations (e.g., singles, couples, families, elderly), and general lifestyle characteristics.
- *Scheduling.* The time schedule is an issue that can make or break the success of the new service. The key factors are the traffic flow (people and automobiles), fellowship needs and expectations, and people's lifestyles.
- *Childcare needs.* A difficult issue to address is when and how to provide necessary childcare. The key factors to consider are ages of children in your church, the expectations of members, and the number of potential childcare workers.
- *Musicians.* Multiple services require additional music teams. The key factor is the availability of current and potential music personnel.

- *Support ministries.* Adding a new worship service requires additional support personnel (e.g., parking attendants, ushers, greeters, refreshment servers). A key factor is the ability to recruit, train, and deploy workers.

Q: I'd like to move toward adding another worship service. How should I proceed?

A: Consider the following ideas as you develop plans for adding another worship service.

- *Start keeping accurate records.* Keep track of worship attendance, the number of cars in the parking lot, and the ratio of children to adults. Especially note when worship attendance approaches 70–80 percent of the seating capacity.
- *Prepare your leaders.* Train your leaders to understand the relationship of seating capacity, parking capacity, and childcare capacity to the overall growth in worship attendance. Suggest a strategy for adding additional services as they are needed.
- *Educate the congregation.* Alert the people to the possibility of adding multiple worship services. Solicit comments through surveys and personal contacts. Research people's preferences in worship style and times for multiple services.
- *Set a target date.* Discern the best time to begin another worship service and begin communicating it to your leaders and congregation well ahead.
- *Recruit and train additional staff.* Start recruiting and training ushers, musicians, childcare workers,

and worship teams. Look for people who are not serving and seek to involve them in support roles.

- *Communicate the opportunity.* Advertise the new worship service to lapsed members, the current congregations, and potential attendees in the community via social media, direct mail, and in-house communication.
- *Experiment for one year.* Promote the new service as a faith experiment. Conduct the additional service for nine to twelve months before performing a full review.

11

DEVELOPING STAFF

Staff for Growth

Q: Our church is growing, and I am no longer able to keep up with the demands of ministry. I see other churches with multiple staff. How vital is it to hire and develop a staff team in my church?

A: Adding pastoral and support staff is an urgent need in a growing church. Throughout most of church history, churches were too small to need more than one pastor. However, as churches have grown larger, the need for additional pastoral and support staff has risen. Observation reveals that a solo pastor can serve between 150 and 200 people well. Unless a second pastor and additional staff are added, a church will plateau at that size. The fact that most churches peak around 200 in worship attendance points out that most churches are staffed for a decline rather than for growth. If you desire the church you lead to grow, you must prepare to add staff. As I always say, staff for growth.

Q: I do desire for my church to grow. Are there any guidelines on how many staff a church needs?

A: The simple answer is that a church needs one full-time pastor and one full-time support staff person for every 150 people in worship attendance. Another way to look at this is a church needs one staff person for every 75 people in attendance. Those numbers offer a solid guide, but the exact number of staff depends on a few factors. For example, more staff are needed if . . .

- the church is program-based
- there are few volunteers
- the pastoral staff are specialists

Fewer staff are needed if . . .

- the church is cell-based
- there are many volunteers
- the pastoral staff are generalists

These guidelines are a good place to start. If a church wants to grow to, say, 300 worshipers, it will need four staff persons (two pastors and two support staff). If it desires to grow to 450 worshipers, it will need six staff persons (three pastors and three support staff).

Staffing for growth means leaders must think ahead to add staff before they're needed. The church of 200 can't wait until it reaches 300 in attendance to add more staff. Adding staff *before* they're needed is what enables the church to grow.

Q: As a solo pastor, I've never hired staff before. Where do I start? How do I know whom to hire?

Developing Staff

A: Adding pastoral and support staff is an urgent need in a growing church. When a church starts growing, the responsibilities on a pastor's desk become even more complex and numerous, which limits the pastor's ability to give adequate emphasis and time to ministry priorities. Begin by evaluating the needs of your church. Divide the church's ministry into six parts:

- Evangelism
- Welcome
- Worship
- Education
- Administration
- Care

Then assess your own strengths. If you are strong in one of the first three areas, look for a new staff person who's strong in one of the second three. Or if you're strong in one of the second three, hire a second staff person whose strength is in one of the first three areas. The idea is to bring balance to the team. Over time, look to fill each of the six areas with pastoral and support staff. In general, your church may need to add staff if it answers yes to any of the following questions:

- Is our church experiencing numerical growth?
- Is our church stuck on a growth plateau?
- Are many things not getting done?
- Do we have difficulty welcoming and involving newer people?
- Are there needs we should be meeting but are not?
- Is our church becoming more complex?

171

- Are there ministry opportunities we'd like to focus on but can't?
- Is the ministry more than the current staff can handle?
- Are we losing worshipers because we're too small?
- Do we desire to move the church in new directions without ending current ministry activities?

The C's of Staffing

Q: Three years ago we hired a new youth pastor, but they never fit into our church and left after fifteen months. We need to do a better job of hiring the next staff person. Help?

A: Hiring pastoral staff is not a new concept. The question is, what should a church look for to bring about an excellent fit between church and staff, as well as staff members with other staff members? The "C process" is an old one, and no one knows for sure where it originated. So here is my take on this approach to determining what to look for in a new pastoral staff member.

- *Call.* Look for a person who has a clear leading to your church and to the open position. Does the person show evidence of self-awareness and the call of God on his or her life? Do they have a passion for ministry that goes beyond seeing this position as just a job?
- *Character.* Look for a person of integrity who is above reproach. Among other things, seek someone who is humble and teachable and (if married) has a solid marriage.

Developing Staff

- *Competence.* Look for a person qualified to do the job. Do their education, experience, and skills fit the position? Do they have a track record of fruitfulness? Have they had success in establishing vision and direction in prior ministry situations?
- *Compass.* Look for a person who has goals in life and ministry and a high degree of emotional and spiritual maturity. Is the individual a lifelong learner? Are they growing spiritually? Is there evidence of spiritual, emotional, and relational growth? Are they heading somewhere or just drifting along?
- *Communication.* Look for a person who has excellent skills in speaking and writing. Do they have a public and private communication style that fits and connects with your people? Are they biblically and theologically articulate?
- *Chemistry.* Look for a person who fits relationally with your congregation and present staff team. Are they an authentic team player? Do they bring energy to the staff team or leave others depressed and discouraged? Are they able to lift others up in ministry and life? Does their personality connect well with those they must work with? Do they have a genuine pastoral heart?
- *Capacity.* Look for a person who can handle the challenges of ministry. Do they demonstrate a strong work ethic, resiliency, stamina, and energy? Are they able to multiply themselves by building teams? Do they delegate well? Can they accept change and lead others to change with diplomacy?
- *Culture.* Look for a person who understands and fits the community and regional culture of your church.

Will their appearance or style preferences build trust or distract from your church's ministry? Can they appropriately engage the many constituents both inside and outside your church?

- *Context.* Look for a person who fits the size, life cycle, and generational context of your church. Do they understand the church's history and life stage? Are they the right person for today's job?

- *Commitment.* Look for a person who can make a long-term commitment to your church. Do they have a track record of longevity in other ministry positions or jobs? Have they stayed long enough in previous work situations to build trust and establish a significant ministry? Do they see your position as a stepping stone to something else?

- *Common sense.* Look for a person who has an ability to perceive, understand, and judge things reasonably. Are they able to reason, converse, and work with others in a wise and reasonable manner?

Nine Principles of Hiring

Q: There must be numerous ways to recruit and hire staff members. What are some basics?

A: Leading a growing church brings numerous challenges. One is learning to hire the right staff. So, here are nine principles for hiring additional staff.

1. *Create a shopping list.* Decide what the position looks like and the knowledge and experience a person needs to do the job. Examine the primary

Developing Staff

responsibilities of the vacated or new position and the areas that will require the most time. With these details in mind, write a profile of the ideal person to fill the position to have a grid established for future evaluation. What specific education is necessary? What vocational background is preferred? What depth of experience is mandated by the role? Determine in advance not to lower your expectations no matter how desperate you feel. Never compare multiple candidates against each other.

2. *Use team interviews.* Every résumé has flaws. Some present a distorted picture and cover up a person's true strengths and weaknesses. Add to this the fact that a candidate can fool a single interviewer and you have the potential for a poor hire. Seldom, however, will a candidate get past a tag-team interview. Choose two or three other people in your church who share your vision and concur with the new job profile. Involve them in the interview process to balance the screening of candidates. This increases internal morale and trust and keeps you from being blindsided later.

3. *Ask specific questions.* Explore several areas by asking targeted questions such as, "Tell me about a time when you felt you did well in a previous job" or "Tell me about a time when you didn't do your best." Such questions reveal strengths and weaknesses of the candidate. Ask about the strengths and weaknesses of previous supervisors to explore the candidate's personal maturity in dealing with authority figures. You might ask, "What was your

major success on your last job? What was your significant failure?" These two questions examine the candidate's ability to accept responsibility versus placing blame. Questions, if designed well, cut to the heart of issues.

4. *Listen well.* After you ask a question, be quiet and let the candidate talk. Most will tell you more than they planned if you are quiet. Intuition plays a role in hiring new staff. If you have a feeling about someone, whether positive or negative, chances are you acquired this feeling from listening. Listen for the use of pronouns. The use of "I" could be a sign of independence. When a candidate speaks in "we" terms, it implies they have used a team concept in the past, which will carry forward.

5. *Take notes.* Interviewers retain around 75 percent of what they hear in an interview. Added to this is the chance of confusing observations when interviewing multiple candidates. It's good to use a checklist based on your profile as an aid in keeping notes. When you seek to narrow down your search, the notes will be helpful.

6. *Seek self-starters.* Many candidates can fulfill a job description but few are motivated to go beyond expectations. Attempt to draw out of the candidate examples of projects they have completed and the results accomplished. Dig into the process they used to get the job done, their work ethic, and what they did when finished. Proven producers always produce. More than that, they have a contagious work ethic. Others follow their model.

7. *Determine passion.* By this I mean what a candidate loves to do and what motivates them in ministry. While most people can complete a task, only those who are passionate gain kingdom satisfaction and renewal. If you desire a new hire to stay with you for a long time, they must serve in an area of their passion. Every organization has clock-watchers who rarely stretch beyond their comfort zone and are unhappy with their position and future. Seek to determine what empowers the candidate.

8. *Evaluate followership.* Sometimes a candidate who has ability, education, and drive may cause you to feel uneasy, but you can't put your finger on why. Only once they have settled in after their initial few weeks on the job do problems arise that were not evident during the interview process. Projects that are not completed become another person's fault. Decisions the person dislikes go unaddressed even as they talk about it behind the leader's back. When hiring a staff member, evaluate their willingness to be a follower. Seek to determine how the person reacts when they disagree with a decision. A penetrating question you could ask is, "What are some things you didn't like about your previous boss and why?"

9. *Establish loyalty.* One of the reasons churches fail to fulfill their mission is the issue of leadership tenure. This has generated a leadership crisis. If the position you seek to fill is vital to the ministry, longevity is a key to effective hiring. Thus, it's important to discover the future needs and aspirations of the candidate. Is there further education on the horizon? How long

will it take for them to become adept and functional in this position? Do they see this position as a short-term stepping stone?

Are there perfect hires? Not on earth! But these principles enable any leader to find the right person who has integrity and passion and is ready to join the team.

Promote from Within or from Without?

Q: There's a great deal of pressure to promote our children's pastor to be our new pastor of family life. I'm a bit concerned. How should I proceed?

A: One issue churches face when hiring staff is the question of whether it is in the best interests of the organization to promote people from within the church or whether they should, from time to time, look outside for new blood.

This is a question that is important for middle-sized to larger congregations. In the last few years, the emphasis has been on promoting from within a church. This is encouraged by leaders who suggest that lifting up people from within the church is the best way to keep the focus on the vision of the church. While this may be true, it is not the only aspect that needs to be considered when promoting leaders.

Here are the basic reasons a church may want to promote from *within*:

1. To maintain the essential DNA of the congregation
2. To reward people for excellent ministry
3. To encourage good people to stay
4. To build long-term loyalty

Developing Staff

5. To keep the church running smoothly
6. To focus on leadership development
7. To preserve continuity

Here are the basic reasons a church may want to promote from *without*:

1. To encourage fresh thinking
2. To eliminate ingrown groupthink
3. To challenge ineffectiveness
4. To discover new models
5. To motivate lazy workers
6. To employ the best people
7. To lift the level of excellence

The Basic Rule

If your church ministry is going well, it is best to promote leaders from within to maintain the good procedures and practices. However, if things are not going so well, it is best to promote from without to encourage fresh ideas, new procedures, and better practices. The basic rule is: If you want things to change, promote from without. If you want things to remain the same, promote from within.

Digging Deeper

One or more of the following issues should be considered when deciding whether to promote from within or without.

1. It is common for outsiders to be resisted or resented. When people are promoted from without, it is normal for insiders to feel like the outsider does not

really understand the church and that they have not worked their way up through the ranks. This, along with the fact that outsiders often receive more pay than insiders, often leads to feelings of resentment. If you promote from without, how do you plan to mitigate the potential ill feelings of insiders?

2. People who have worked in direct ministry areas have often developed skills that are effective in relational ministry, but they may not have the skills to be effective in management. Simply because a person is fruitful at one level of ministry does not mean he or she will be effective at another level. If you promote from within, how will you determine if a person has the skill set to lead and manage at a higher level?

3. If a church never brings in people from outside, there is a danger of becoming ingrown and developing senior leaders who resist change. If you promote from within, how will you overcome these challenges?

4. To maintain unity within the church, it is crucial to educate leaders on the different roles that people fill and the gifts that they bring. How are you helping current leaders understand the need for people with different gifts and the necessity of having gifted people in the church?

5. Churches only grow as leaders grow. How are you training leaders to grow in their present and future areas of responsibility?

6. It helps to maintain morale if leaders clearly understand potential career paths in your church. Have you analyzed and described potential

career paths for your current leaders? How are you communicating and training leaders for potential promotions?

7. As people are promoted, it is helpful if they receive a new title that communicates to others that things have changed. In today's church climate where equality of people and calling is highlighted, how are you communicating that some leaders have greater responsibility than others?

Staff Development

There are four different causes that give rise to leadership and leaders.

1. *Crisis need.* A crisis arises in a church or other organization. Someone notices the crisis and steps up to take charge of the situation. The person may never have thought of themselves as a leader, but they respond to the need of the moment and in doing so discover an ability to lead others.

2. *Perceived inequity.* An individual perceives an inequity among different groups of people. It might be differences related to gender, age, economics, ethnicity, or other aspects of social life. Their response is to move into leadership to right a perceived wrong.

3. *Personal challenge.* A leader offers a dynamic challenge to a wide audience to get involved. The challenge comes with a "throw them up against the wall to see if they stick" training. Some people respond to this emotional call and become effective leaders, but others flame out in discouragement.

4. *Search for excellence.* A leader communicates a clear vision of leadership development. The desire to raise up new leaders is tied to a strong vision of the future of the church or organization. A clear process of recruiting, training, deploying, and supporting new leaders is designed and implemented.

As you think about your church or organization, which of the four causes do you see at work? How have most leaders been discovered in your context?

12

FINISHING WELL

Leadership Risks in Ministry

Q: I love being a pastor, but it's tiring. Other people in my church don't appear to face the same challenges I do. Are there unique aspects of leadership pastors face that make us so tired?

A: After nearly nine years in pastoral ministry, I found myself struggling with having enough energy to do the job. Each day I would go into my office, shut the door, and promptly fall asleep on the couch. No doubt people in the outer offices detected the silence and assumed I was praying. They were right to one extent. I was praying . . . for a new place of ministry that would refresh my energy level. The years of sermon prep, pastoral care, handling conflict, and leading change had taken a toll. When I first came to this church, I wore a clean white tunic (so to speak). However, after nine years of making changes, dealing with upset parishioners, and facing numerous issues large and small, my tunic was quite stained. Stained, in fact, to the point that I could no longer lead. I eventually moved on to a new place of ministry that provided fresh challenges and opportunities for my personal growth and development.

Looking back on those days, I now recognize I was battling with the two main reasons pastors change ministry: vision conflict and compassion fatigue.

Vision Conflict

Vision conflict is a relatively new concept, although the essential aspects have been around as long as pastoral ministry has existed. Simply put, vision conflict refers to the difference between what pastors expect to happen when they enter ministry and what actually happens.

When a pastor experiences a call to ministry, it is natural to develop expectations about what that ministry will be like. For example, it's common for younger pastors to see themselves spending nearly all week studying the text of Scripture in preparation to preach on Sunday. Disparity arises as they discover ministry is constructed around high demands and numerous meetings, which may keep them away from the study of Scripture. Such vision conflict between what they expect and the reality of ministry often results in feelings of self-doubt and fear.

Compassion Fatigue

Compassion fatigue is better understood than vision conflict. Spiritual fatigue, compassion stress, and emotional labor are other terms used to describe the same phenomenon. Compassion fatigue is the depletion of emotional, spiritual,

Finishing Well

and physical energy that a pastor experiences when taking on too much of other people's burdens. It can demonstrate itself in a few maladies, but depression and persistent exhaustion are common. The presence of compassion fatigue among pastors is to be expected; indeed, it is inevitable. Pastors serve in a role that has a high-low liability. For example, an emotional high at worship on Sunday morning may be followed within a few minutes or hours by an emotional low when a church member complains because their needs were not met as expected.

Fatigue also comes as pastors shepherd others through times of high trauma, like the death of a loved one, which may leave pastors depleted of their own spiritual and emotional reserves. And given the reality that pastors serve the very people they also rely on for their own spiritual and emotional support, it is easy to see how this dual relationship results in fatigue.

FACING THE FACTS

Are you experiencing vision conflict or compassion fatigue? While the following questionnaire is not perfect, it will give you basic insight into your current situation.

For each statement below, respond *yes* or *no*.

1. I feel overworked.	Yes	No
2. My sense of confidence is diminished.	Yes	No
3. My trust in church leaders is weak.	Yes	No
4. I question my calling as a pastor.	Yes	No
5. My life is far too stressful.	Yes	No
6. I feel my work is futile.	Yes	No
7. I feel isolated and alone.	Yes	No

8. My board and I disagree on the vision of the church. Yes No
9. I feel emotionally empty. Yes No
10. I am confused about my major role. Yes No
11. My spouse and family are unhappy. Yes No
12. I am not working in my area of giftedness. Yes No
13. My work is too demanding. Yes No
14. I am insecure in my present position. Yes No
15. I must prove myself a hard worker. Yes No
16. My ministry is not satisfying. Yes No
17. It is difficult for me to say no. Yes No
18. My dream of success has not happened. Yes No
19. I can't meet the needs of my people. Yes No
20. I would like to leave my church. Yes No

If you responded *yes* to ten or more statements, you are likely facing either vision conflict or compassion fatigue.

Are more of your *yes* responses on the odd numbered statements? Then you are facing compassion fatigue. If more of your *yes* responses are on the even numbered statements, you are struggling with vision conflict. Why not talk about your answers with someone you trust?

Moving to a New Church

Q: *For the last couple of years, I've had a sense that my ministry is finished in this church. A few of my ministry heroes stayed a lifetime in their churches, but I feel it's time to leave my present church. What issues do I need to consider in making a good decision?*

A: Pastors don't like to think of their present church ministry as a stepping stone to another one. However, while some pastors remain in the same church for decades, the reality is that every year there are pastors who move from church to church.

When is it time to move on? It can be difficult to determine when to call it quits and when to stay put. Before throwing in the proverbial towel, take time to assess your situation. Here are some questions to ask and answer truthfully before deciding to leave or stay.

- *Do you have unfinished goals?* Pastors often take positions because they can see a clear vision pathway for improvement of a particular ministry. Once they accomplish the vision or goals they had in mind, it's natural to feel restless. You need to ask questions like, "Where do I want my ministry to be in five years? In ten years?" If you have finished your goals and cannot discover an exciting new vision for the future, it might be time to move on to a ministry that excites you more.
- *Do you have learning opportunities available?* Pastors usually take ministry positions that provide challenges and opportunities for personal growth. After serving in a ministry for several years, some feel that they've mastered the job and start to feel less challenged. Does your church ministry provide for study leave, professional development, or financial help to obtain the services of a coach? If so, it might be best to stay and take hold of the growth opportunities that are available. However, if your ministry does not support learning options for you, it might be time to move on.
- *Do you have productive working relationships?* Human resource specialists say that people remain

in a job based on the quality of workplace relationships. Pastors know that it's certainly easier to work with some people more than others. If working with some people is affecting the quality of your work, it may be time to act by negotiating better working relationships. If the personal dynamics do not get better, it might be time to move on to a new ministry.

- *Do you have a healthy working environment?* When you wake up in the morning, are you excited to go to work? Do you look forward to your daily tasks, or do you feel stressed to the point that it's not fun anymore? If the stress is so great that it's affecting the quality of your life, you need to see if you can change your workday patterns to create a more relaxed environment. Talk with those who oversee your work and see if you can reduce your load, find more resources, or eliminate demands. If you can't find a way to design a healthier work environment, it might be time to move on to a new ministry.

- *Do you find the quality of your work satisfying?* Pastors, perhaps more than others, like to feel they are making a difference in people's lives as well as in the life of the entire church. Thus, it's important that you sense the work you are doing is contributing to important change in the world. If your role and contribution are not personally significant, it is wise to consider the options for a change within your current ministry. If that is not possible, then it might be time to move on to a new ministry.

- *Do you feel valued and appreciated?* While pastors do not serve for recognition, everyone desires to have some level of appreciative feedback. If your church or ministry doesn't provide regular feedback or recognition, give some thought to what you'd like to see happen. How would you like to be appropriately rewarded, recognized, or noted? Talk to the board or other leaders to see if some process for demonstrating appreciation can be set up. If some system for recognition, reward, or appreciation cannot be designed, it might be time to move on to a new ministry.

- *Do you need more time to be effective?* How long have you been in your present ministry? Studies continue to demonstrate that ministry effectiveness usually takes place following six to seven years of faithful ministry. The most difficult year often is year six, but if you stay and work strategically, ministry turns around in year seven. So, if you've been in your ministry less than six years, it's usually best to remain another year or two to see what changes. However, if you've served seven or more years without fruitfulness, it might be time to move on to a new ministry.

Is it time to move on? Thinking through each of those questions may give you fresh insights to inform what is a very personal decision.

Changing Careers

Q: My ministry hasn't gone as well as I hoped, and I wonder if I should change careers?

A: Pastors don't like to think of ministry as a career. Yet, some aspects of pastoral ministry are similar to a career, and it's wise to give heed to practical aspects of changing roles, locations, or, yes, even a complete change of career.

Two Types of Calling

Pastors tend to think of their calling in two parts: *general call* and *specific call*. A general call to ministry implies that a pastor feels called to make their financial living from the gospel, while a specific call implies a pastor feels called to serve in a definite role, location, or position. While a general call to ministry may not change for most pastors, it's common for a specific call to change throughout a lifetime of ministry, with pastors often having three to six specific calls over their lifetime.

Life Changes

Centuries ago, it was common for a pastor to experience a general call and a specific call as one. In the 1700s, it was rare for pastors to change churches in their lifetime. Travel was not easy and fewer ministry roles existed. Travel today is easier, of course, and there are numerous and various opportunities for ministry.

Life change impacts ministry in other ways too. A ministry position that once appeared perfect may now seem all wrong. Pastors may need a change due to family situations, or perhaps they've outgrown their current role or desire to pursue new interests.

Some pastors just fell into their positions at some point without much thought. Now, after ten to twenty years of experience, they find themselves stuck in an ill-fitting position with no satisfaction in what they're doing.

Changing a General Call

Let's consider for a moment the major challenge of a complete career change—that is, a change in the general call of ministry.

If you feel you've made a mistake in understanding your general call (career), it's important to take some time *now* to think about who you are and what your gifts and passions are. Here are some things to consider . . .

Valid Reasons to Change

- You've been haunted for years by a vision or passion for work outside of traditional pastoral ministry.
- You don't fit in ministry positions even though you've tried for years.
- Your love for ministry is not there and you dislike going to work.
- You've been fired or let go from ministry positions two or more times.
- Your values are not in sync with ministry work.

Invalid Reasons to Change

- Your motivation is security or money.
- You've experienced a bruised ego and are hurt.
- A friend or relative has a fabulous or lucrative career you could join.
- You're tired or burned out.
- You're running away from problems that are likely to surface in a new career.

In short, you shouldn't jump careers just because you're facing tough times or fantasizing about a different position. Prior to making a major change, evaluate your general call to ministry.

- Spend personal time in prayer asking God to guide you.
- Talk and listen to close family members and key friends.
- Find a ministry or life coach to walk with you as you consider a change.

Charting a New Direction

Once you determine a career change is in order, it's then time to consider a new calling or career. Put the following ideas into practice to help chart the future.

1. *Explore a no-fail dream.* If you're going to change careers, you might as well try to find the most exciting option. So, if you knew you couldn't fail in your next career, what would you do?
   - Put your dream career on paper. For the greatest impact, take a legal pad and write out your ideas by hand. Putting words on paper will help you process your thoughts better than typing on a computer or tablet.
   - Write out thoughts, including the kind of work you would do, where you would live, how much you would earn, your typical day, your surroundings, what you would wear, and other ideas that occur to you. Think about your personality and

what makes you thrive, feel alive, and challenged. Would you work alone or on a team? In a large company or a small one? Live in a big city or a smaller one? Be in a high-pressure environment or a relaxed one? Have a flexible schedule or standard hours? Travel or be at home?

- Ask yourself the following two questions: (1) What elements of my dream career are not found in my current ministry role? (2) Which two elements must I have in my next career to be happy and fulfilled? Your answers to these two questions are the core elements.

2. *Interpret your findings.* Look at your core elements and think about them broadly. How do you understand them? The better you can interpret your own core elements, the closer you'll be to finding a new career.

3. *Create a list of your skills.* On a piece of paper, list the skills you use well in your current position. For example: recruiting volunteers, organizing events, public speaking. Add other skills you are good at but perhaps don't have opportunity to use in your current position. When finished, put a star next to the skills that bring you the most satisfaction.

4. *Determine possible positions.* Look over your no-fail dream, its core elements, and the list of skills you do well. Talk to others, describe your skills and core elements, and inquire about what positions might fit them. A key question to ask is "Who earns a living doing something like I've described?" Search the internet for information about careers

that use your core elements and skills. Determine three to five possible positions, companies, or fields that appear to fit you.

5. *Network, network, network.* Changing careers today is more about networking than writing a résumé. Now, you will need a résumé, but speak with people in the fields you are interested in. Ask questions, find out what each opportunity involves, narrow it down to one or two choices, and test the waters. Doing so will lead you to a fresh opportunity that may be a better career (general call) for you.

When to Leave

Q: I've enjoyed my ministry life but am getting to the point of retirement. How do I know when it's time to leave?

A: Some pastors point out that the concept of retirement is not found in the Bible. Others note that vacations are not found in the Bible either, but it's still wise to take them. All, of course, agree that God expects us to be guided by wisdom.

Peak Years of Ministry

Studies of peak performance have been completed for several professions. For example, professional athletes tend to peak around age 28, and the average age for those setting world records in athletics is 26.[1] Of course, some Olympic medal winners have been over forty, and a few well-known football, baseball, and basketball players have competed into their forties.

---

1. Erik Malinowski, "For Athletes' Peak Performance, Age Is Everything," *Wired*, July 12, 2011, https://www.wired.com/2011/07/athletes-peak-age/.

Finishing Well

For careers that involve mental creativity, performance tends to peak later in life. Philip Hans Franses, an economist, found that physicists have often made their most important discoveries at age 48, while chess grand masters tend to peak in their mental acuity at age 31. Famous artists have produced their most priceless works around age 42, Nobel Prize–winning authors most often wrote their best work at age 45, and classical composers have written their most popular music at 39. The average age for a person's prime creative work is 42.[2]

If the general studies of creative people in similar occupations holds true for pastors, most will reach their peak creativity between 35 and 50 years of age. But, like in other professions, some pastors will continue to minster effectively well into their eighties.

Why Pastors Stay Too Long

Pastors often wait too long to retire for a number of reasons, but here are a few that top the list.

- *A lack of financial preparation for retirement.* Today's churches usually try to help a pastor save financially for retirement, but that was not so common just twenty years ago. Many pastors continue to minister beyond their prime simply because they need to keep earning money.
- *People are healthier today.* Some pastors are physically rigorous in their sixties and feel that they can

2. Betsy Mikel, "This Is the Peak Age for Creativity, Science Says," *Inc.*, September 13, 2016, https://www.inc.com/betsy-mikel/this-is-the-peak-age-for-creativity-science-says.html.

pastor well into their mid-seventies. They like to say that seventy-five is the new sixty-five.

- *Their calling is not finished.* Pastors surmise their years of experience have made them more qualified to pastor, so why quit?
- *They don't want to lose the social benefits of pastoring.* The respect of having people look to them for leadership, care, and assistance is difficult to give up.

Signs It's Time to Retire

Deciding when to leave pastoral ministry is a complex decision. Here are some things to consider.

- *Your health.* Are you and your spouse in good health? What is the history of longevity in your family? Take these matters seriously. Delaying retirement could mean you won't be able to do what you'd like in the future.
- *Your money.* The standard rule of thumb is that your savings, investments, and social security need to equal twenty-five times the annual amount you need to live in retirement. If that is not true for you, you may need to work longer.
- *Your future.* You need to retire *to* something, not just *from* something. Answering three questions will help you determine if it's time to retire:
  1. What do I want to do?
  2. Where do I want to do it?
  3. Who do I want to do it with?
- *Your ministry.* Are you able to lead your church into the future? Are you capable of casting vision for the

next decade? If you find yourself just coasting along, perhaps it's time to leave the stage.

Ending Well

Q: *Every day it seems I hear of another pastor or church leader failing in ministry. It's heartbreaking. What do I need to do to keep it from happening to me too?*

A: A study by J. Robert Clinton of leaders described in the Bible reveals only around 30 percent of them finished well.[3] Of course, we know more about some leaders in the Bible than others. For about half of the leaders mentioned in Scripture, we have enough information to place them in one of the following four categories, which can also be applied to ministry leaders:

1. *Some leaders were cut off early in their lives.* They were taken out of leadership in several ways (e.g., assassinated, overthrown, killed in battle).
2. *Some leaders finished poorly.* Such leaders often declined in skill, competence, or relationship with God.
3. *Some leaders finished so-so.* They did not accomplish what they could have or should have done.
4. *Some leaders finished well.* They continued to walk closely with God and accomplished his purposes.

All leaders face a time (or times) in their lives when they must make a decision (or decisions) that impact them for the

---

3. J. Robert Clinton, "Listen Up Leaders! Some Thoughts on Biblical Leaders and Finishing Well" (Barnabas Publishers Reprint, 1989), 2, https://clintonleadership.com/resources/complimentary/ListenUpLeaders.pdf.

rest of their lives. A leader typically faces one to three major pivot points in their life. Each leader's response to God's work in their life marks their ministry for years to come. The pivot point(s) can lead to one of three eventualities:

- *End the use of the leader for God's purposes.* They are no longer trusted enough to continue serving in a ministry leadership role.
- *Curtail the leader's work.* Their usefulness for God's work is diminished or at least their potential is limited.
- *Enhance the leader's contribution to the ultimate purposes of God's kingdom.* Their decision builds trust and gives evidence of internal integrity for continued and expanded ministry.

In Psalm 90, Moses reminds us to "number our days" that we may present to God a heart of wisdom (v. 12). Like Moses, Christian leaders must seek to finish well so our life isn't wasted because of our human mistakes. I conclude by sharing some principles that will enable you to finish well.

- *Study biblical leaders to understand how God worked through them.* The writer of Hebrews reminds us, "Remember your leaders, those who spoke to you the word of God. Consider the outcome of their way of life and imitate their faith. Jesus Christ is the same yesterday and today and forever" (13:7–8 ESV). By accessing the lessons learned from past leaders—both positive and negative—we can discover how to finish well.
- *Build renewal experiences into your life.* Leaders who finish well experience times of renewal. Such times

are important in one's mid-thirties to mid-fifties (often called a midlife crisis); however, pastors need to renew or reinvent themselves every seven to ten years. Without such renewal, Christian leaders tend to plateau in life and ministry, and there is usually a sense of confusion regarding achievement and future direction. Being open to God's renewing and initiating personal times of renewal are important aspects of finishing well.

- *Guard your inner life.* In his late sixties and nearing the end of his life, the apostle Paul encouraged Timothy, "Train yourself for godliness; for while bodily training is of some value, godliness is of value in every way" (1 Tim. 4:7–8 ESV). Leaders must assess their spiritual lives on a regular basis. Godly habits can shape character and increase one's potential for finishing well.

- *Maintain a learning posture all your life.* In Paul's final words to Timothy, he tells him to bring "the books" (2 Tim. 4:13). Paul was still learning late in life. Maintaining a learning posture usually involves reading. Of course, participating in other learning activities will help you finish well too.

- *Establish relationships with mentors.* One thing church leaders who have finished well have in common is that they have mentors who can speak into their lives. Find and meet with a person who can help you finish well.

WRAPPING UP

The pace of change increases each year. We see it everywhere we look, from technology to business to education. It's also observable in the roles and practices of pastors.

The biblical functions, of course, aren't changing. Pastors preach the Word, evangelize the lost, care for souls, shepherd the flock, and perform a host of other duties. Yet, how they carry out such biblical functions varies along with the ever-changing forces in our culture.

The Ministry Answer Book for Pastors is a guide to serving God's people in changing times. While it addresses typical duties like conducting funerals, it also covers modern concerns such as leading a church board.

If you are a pastor or a leader of a church, keep this book close at hand. You'll find it a welcome resource to answer the questions we're facing in our changing world.

But you, be sober in all things, endure hardship, do the work of an evangelist, fulfill your ministry. (2 Tim. 4:5)

GARY L. MCINTOSH is a prominent figure in the field of church growth, having authored numerous books and articles on the subject. His work focuses on practical and strategic approaches to helping churches expand and thrive.

McIntosh serves as distinguished affiliate professor of Christian Ministry and Leadership (retired) at Talbot School of Theology, Biola University. He is a professor in the Talbot Doctor of Ministry program where he co-leads the Growing and Multiplying Churches cohort and serves as a dissertation mentor.

A key theme in McIntosh's work is the concept of intentional growth, suggesting that churches can develop and flourish by engaging their communities, equipping their members, and adapting to changing cultural landscapes. He also emphasizes the importance of understanding the unique characteristics and needs of a local congregation when formulating growth strategies.

McIntosh is known for providing practical and actionable insights, often drawing from his extensive experience in church consulting and leadership development. His work aims to equip church leaders with the tools and knowledge needed to foster growth, deepen spiritual impact, and create vibrant, healthy church communities.

Overall, Gary McIntosh's contributions to the field of church growth emphasize the significance of intentional, strategic approaches that are firmly rooted in a deep understanding of the dynamics of church life and the needs of the people they serve.

Dr. McIntosh has forty-two years of experience consulting nonprofit organizations, coaching leaders, and seminar presentations. He has analyzed numerous churches representing some 90+ denominations throughout the United States, Canada, Australia, and Southeast Asia.

Gary and his wife, Carol, reside in Temecula, California. They have two grown sons, nine grandchildren, and four great-grandchildren. Dr. McIntosh is available for speaking, teaching, or consulting.

Connect with Gary for more information and to register to receive his leadership newsletter "Ready, Set, Grow!"

 www.ChurchGrowthNetwork.com

 @GaryLMcIntosh

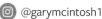 @garymcintosh1

 @drgmcintosh